The Third World in World Economy

Previously Published

The Pillage of the Third World

Pierre Jalée

The Third World in World Economy

Translated from the French
by Mary Klopper

New York and London

*I dedicate this book to the
Organization for the Solidarity of the
Peoples of Africa, Asia, and Latin America*

Contents

2

Descriptive Economic Indices for Major Countries   145

Introduction

The attention paid to my earlier book, *The Pillage of the Third World*,[1] both in French and in translation, showed that the subject matter filled a gap in the knowledge of many of my contemporaries. Yet there is already an abundance of writing on the Third World. It appeared, however, that to study the economic relations between the Third World and the advanced capitalist nations—taking each of these groups as a single entity —was, if not to open up an entirely original field of research, to explore little known territory. When one enters such territory one is naturally tempted to push on as far as possible while opening up the field and making it more accessible.

This is the purpose of the present work, which is in a direct line of descent from the earlier one. It contains more advanced documentary and statistical research and, in consequence, so many figures that I thought it best to present almost all of them in full-page tables at the ends of chapters. The field of investigation is also larger: The subject of the chapter dealing with agriculture has been extended to cover animal husbandry and fisheries, the chapter dealing with the products of the sub-soil includes energy, etc. On the other hand, I have done justice to my title by not only comparing the Third World with that composed of advanced capitalist states, but also by setting out the data for the socialist countries whenever they were available.

To regard the Third World as a single economic entity is, I know, in one sense schematic and arbitrary. But I also know that in a much more important sense this reflects the fundamental

[1] *The Pillage of the Third World* (New York and London: Monthly Review Press, 1968).

reality. Underneath the differences between their natural resources and level of development, the underdeveloped countries of Latin America, Asia, and Africa have in common the fundamental characteristics of economies complementary to those of the advanced capitalist countries. The pillage to which they are subjected is the profound reality common to them all. Nevertheless, throughout the analysis I have tried to differentiate between them fairly systematically, by dividing them into sub-groups whose geographical criteria correspond in a general way to economic variations. And in the second part of the book I have set out a sort of table of descriptive economic indices for six socialist countries, for the five most important advanced capitalist countries, and for some fifty of the most characteristic Third World countries; simple but essential data by which comparisons can be made.

I have said that the present work is the child of *The Pillage of the Third World,* but I mean the offspring to pursue and extend the work of the parent, not to repeat it. Unless it is essential to the development of an argument I shall, therefore, avoid repeating what has already been said. When necessary, I shall simply refer to the earlier book.

As I said, this work made it necessary to cite a lot of figures. Most of these have been drawn directly from international publications, a few from national statistics. The source is always given as precisely as possible, as is the period or year to which the figures apply. Although such rigorous documentation is not as common as one might suppose, I consider it essential. It will, of course, be possible to contest any conclusions and perspectives I may reach on the grounds of the logic and the hypotheses I have used, but not on the basis of the statistical data which provide the point of departure.

But what figures should one select? Preferably the most recent. However, I did not think all should be sacrificed to include the most recent figures at any price. And in fact it would not have been possible. The book has required more than a year's work and the statistical investigation preceded the analysis. Moreover, the figures presented here have often been collected or even calculated by the author from the data in a variety of official publications. So it was not possible to prepare the work in a general way

and then, just as it was going to the printer, insert the latest figures hastily drawn from the most recent publications. In short,
all this means that in a number of cases, by the time this book
appears figures more recent by at least one year will have been
issued. This discrepancy does not seem to me unacceptable. Unfortunately, it is also true that many of the publications I have
used for reference themselves give figures which go back two years
from their publication date.[2]

However, there is nothing I can do about this nor, I think, can
the publishers. It is surely better to end up with figures three years
old but analyzed and arranged to give them their maximum significance than to use the latest figures set out anyhow.

Further, though my figures often give a snapshot of a particular
situation at a given moment, I have been at pains to present such
pictures only as the last image of a film covering five, ten, or
fifteen years, and to follow a development by using indices or
percentages or the actual figures of production, trade, or capital
movement at different points in time—changes indicative of a
trend are the most important. If a trend has shown up over a number of years one regrets less that the last observation should have
been made in 1964 instead of 1965, or 1965 instead of 1966.

---

[2] This is particularly the case for the United Nations yearbooks, which
are usually published in the middle of the year following that appearing in
the title and at best give figures for the year preceding that in the title.

1

Chapter I

Basic Data

Before entering into details it may be useful to give some general information to open up the subject.

In the first place, what countries should be included under the heading "Third World"? I hold that the fundamental division in the world is between the countries with a capitalist system and those with a socialist system. But it is generally recognized that there is a wide gulf between the underdeveloped and subject countries and the developed and dominant countries within the capitalist group. The mass of underdeveloped and subject countries dependent on the capitalist system are currently described as the underdeveloped nations of Asia, Africa, and Latin America—for which the common man uses the popular expression "Third World."

The United Nations experts make the same distinctions by dividing the world into "countries with planned economies" (socialist) and "countries with market economies" (capitalist), and by subdividing the latter into "developed countries with market economies" and "developing countries with market economies." Thus the basis of my classification is not particularly novel, but the boundaries between my groups are not exactly those recognized by others. I shall use the following groupings:

COUNTRIES FORMING THE SOCIALIST SYSTEM

U.S.S.R., the People's Democracies of Europe (including Yugoslavia), China, Mongolia, North Korea, North Vietnam, Cuba.

COUNTRIES FORMING THE CAPITALIST SYSTEM

1. *Developed Countries*
   U.S.A., Canada, Europe (excluding the U.S.S.R. and the

3

People's Democracies), Japan, Israel, Australia and New Zealand.
2. *Underdeveloped Countries, or the Third World*
    America (excluding the United States, Canada, and Cuba),
the whole of Africa, Asia (excluding the socialist countries, Japan,
and Israel), Oceania (excluding Australia and New Zealand).

There are always thorny problems of demarcation. Some people
would be astonished that no African country appears in the list of
socialist countries. But whatever sympathy one may have for some
of the countries of that continent, socialism is here taken to be
Marxist and scientific and cannot be Arab or African. Many will
resent the presence of Yugoslavia in the socialist group and I
resent it myself. What could one do? It would be indefensible to
place it in either of the other categories and absurd to make it
into a fourth. Moreover, let us not jump to conclusions, perhaps
the people of Yugoslavia still have something to say.

Other problems arise. Consultation with members of the Turkish
Workers' Party confirmed my intention to include Turkey in the
Third World (although a member of the OECD). South Africa has
also been kept in the Third World—though without consulting
Mr. Vorster—because this seems the only category for a country
where the one-fifth of the inhabitants who enjoy a very high
standard of living are not regarded by the four-fifths whose income
is six times less as subjectively part of the nation and its social
structure.[1]

With its possible imperfections and its obvious borderline cases,
the Third World adopted here is defined—in relation to the world
and to the two other groups of countries, in population and in
area—in Table I-1. It covers 51 percent of the world's dry land
and in 1965 held 46.9 percent of its population. Its population
is growing faster than that of the other countries and the time
must, therefore, be very near when that proportion will reach the
50 percent mark. The Third World can thus be regarded as en-
compassing just about half the population and land area of the
world. It will be noticed that the population of the socialist coun-

---

[1] United Nations documents have adopted the opposite solution and South
Africa is the only important difference between the Third World as used
here and the United Nations group of "developing countries with market
economies." This is noted in my statistical tables when necessary.

tries is exactly one-third of the world total while that of the developed capitalist countries amounts to barely one-fifth.

The Third World is heavily, but very unevenly, populated. Almost two-thirds of its inhabitants are in Asia, while Africa holds only 20 percent and Latin America 15 percent. And if large areas of the Third World are underpopulated, Southeast Asia is, on the other hand, overpopulated. The population density of India, although high, is of the order of 165 inhabitants per square kilometer.

Since it is one of the aspects by which it is defined, everyone knows that the Third World is underdeveloped.[2] To what degree is this so? The specialized chapters will provide a more detailed analysis of the problems but, in the meantime, a few more general indicators of economic development are set out in Table I-2.

Giving the per capita national income in dollars is a very rough approach for countries other than those of the advanced capitalist group. The results for the socialist countries are, in fact, sometimes surprising, mainly because of more or less arbitrary conversion rates and because of a concern with "gross product" rather than with national income. For the Third World it is certainly very restrictive to use only five countries, however carefully selected, to indicate the condition of a continent. However, taking these reservations into account, the figures give a sufficiently graphic picture of the differences between the chosen groups of countries as regards per capita national income. It is worth noting simply that the socialist countries (excluding those in Asia) enjoy a per capita national income about one-third lower than that in the advanced capitalist countries. The inhabitants of the Asian and African countries of the Third World, for their part, have an individual income about one-tenth to one-eleventh that of the inhabitants of the advanced capitalist countries, while that of the Latin Americans comes to about one-fifth. It must not be forgotten

---

[2] I criticized the expression "Third World" in the introduction to *The Pillage of the Third World*. For his part, Charles Bettelheim sets out a most convincing criticism of the term "underdeveloped country" in Chapter 3 of *Planification et Croissance accelérée* (Paris: François Maspero, 1967). But however inadequate or even misleading they may be, some terms are used so universally that it becomes impossible to avoid them. My criticism of the first, nevertheless, remains unchanged, and I accept Dr. Bettelheim's dissatisfaction with the second.

that such national averages take no account of internal disparities. These are small for the socialist countries but, on the other hand, very considerable in some Third World countries where a bourgeoisie of millionaires has arisen alongside poverty-stricken masses whose per capita income gives an inadequate indication of their deplorably low standard of living (India, Latin America).

For all these reasons, greater weight should be given to the more accurate figures indicating per capita consumption of energy and industrial steel. These give a reasonably sure measure of the degree of industrialization and hence of the level of development. Under this heading the African countries of the Third World are appallingly far behind, with those of Asia little better off. The closeness of these two groups of countries shows that in this area they have traversed only about one-twentieth of the course already behind the industrial capitalist countries. The position of the Latin American countries is distinctly better, although they have reached only one-sixth (energy) and one-ninth (industrial steel) of the consumption of the developed capitalist countries.

One might suppose that social development is simply the projection of economic development onto another plane. The data in Table I-3 show that a distinction must be made. In this respect it can first be seen that the socialist countries of Europe are better off than the advanced capitalist countries except in the matter of the spread of ownership of radios: this is simply a reflection of the different objectives of the two systems. It can also be seen that while the Third World countries of Asia and Africa are outdistanced by the advanced capitalist countries in the fields of medicine, broadcasting, and book production, the Third World as a whole is not so far behind in education (columns 2 and 3). Certainly these gross figures are only quantitative measures and it is widely known that the education handed out in the majority of Third World countries is far from satisfactory. This can be seen by comparing columns 2 and 3. There prove to be proportionately more students enrolled than teachers to teach them in Third World countries, which indicates that classes are overloaded or even that two classes are taught part-time by one teacher. It is worth noting that a praiseworthy priority effort in education has, nevertheless, been made by the majority of Third World countries.

This effort was made with means whose inadequacy can be seen from an analysis of the gross domestic product of the world's nations as set out in Table I-4. It seems likely that the estimates in this table are very close to the actual 1965 data for the advanced capitalist countries and for the Third World, but that they are less accurate for the socialist countries. In general the table gives a close enough idea of the absolute and relative economic weight of each of the three groups of countries considered and a reasonably accurate idea of the relationship of forces in this area between the Third World and the group of advanced capitalist countries.

From all this it appears that in 1965 almost half of the world's inhabitants (the Third World) enjoyed only an 11.5 percent share of the world's total gross domestic product, while one-fifth of the world's population (the advanced capitalist countries) took about 60 percent. Six hundred and fifty million human beings produce five times the wealth generated by 1,550 million others. The gross domestic product of the United States alone (population about 195 million) is nearly two and one-half times that of all the underdeveloped countries of Asia, Africa, and Latin America, which have eight times the population. Therefore it seems that, despite some imperfections, this is the most accurate measure so far; it is also the most significant, because of its all-embracing character, and the one which reflects most pitilessly the inequality ruling our world.

There is also inequality inside the Third World—inequality in poverty. Latin America appears to be relatively less poor, with a gross domestic product of $77 billion for 235 million inhabitants. Africa is more than twice as poor, with $50 billion for 310 million inhabitants. But underdeveloped Asia, which produced only $103 billion for almost a billion people, is unspeakably the worst off.[3]

---

[3] In the December 1966 issue of the magazine *Finance and Development,* published by the International Monetary Fund and the World Bank, K. S. Sundara Rajan notes that the per capita gross domestic product of the underdeveloped countries of Asia only comes to one-fortieth of that of the United States and that the "*increase* in goods and services which becomes available to the average United States citizen in a single year is more than

It should be noted in passing that although the gross domestic product of the Third World may have increased in absolute value from 1958 to 1965, it has dropped from 12 percent to 11.5 percent of world production. Changes in the indices of gross domestic product for groups of countries and the annual growth rate for the period 1950 to 1964–65 are given in Table I-5. The data confirm that over this fifteen-year period economic growth has been much more rapid in the socialist countries of Europe than in the advanced capitalist countries but that, taking overall figures for the whole period, this growth has been very similar in the latter group and in the Third World. However, Part B of this table shows that growth has not been uniform. While the advanced capitalist countries, for example, achieved higher growth rates in the latter part of the period, the reverse applies to the Third World.

Not only does the Third World show a terrifying degree of economic backwardness in relation to the advanced countries with the same capitalist system, but the statistical data all tend to suggest that this backwardness has grown relatively worse in recent years, especially as regards per capita growth. The few more recent figures which it has been possible to collect do not allow us to hope that this trend is being reversed.

One conclusion follows: the wave of political independence which swept over the Third World after the Second World War has so far generally not enabled it to overcome its economic backwardness. I shall not yet try to analyze the reasons for this since they should become apparent as the areas of production, trade, and the movement of capital are investigated in the chapters that follow.

---

twice the *total* goods and services at the disposal of the average Asian citizen."

Table I-I

Population and Area in 1965

	Millions of inhabitants	Estimated annual rate of increase (%)	Area in 1000 sq. km.	Population density per sq. km.
World	**3,285**	**1.8**	**135,773**	**24**
Socialist countries				
Europe	122	1.0	1,273	95
U.S.S.R.	231	1.5	22,402	10
China	700	1.5	9,561	72
North Korea	12	3.0	121	98
North Vietnam	19	3.4	159	120
Mongolia	1	2.9	1,535	1
Cuba	8	2.1	115	70
	1,093 (33.3%)		35,166 (26%)	
Developed capitalist countries				
U.S. and Canada	214	1.6	19,340	11
Europe, excluding the socialist countries	322	0.9	3,656	88
Japan	98	1.0	370	265
Israel	3	3.6	21	130
Australia and New Zealand	14	2.1	7,955	2
	651 (19.8%)		31,342 (23%)	
Third World countries				
America, excluding the U.S.A., Canada, Cuba	235	3.0	22,608	10
All Africa	310	2.5	30,258	10
Asia, excluding Japan, Israel, the socialist countries*	992	2.4	15,844	63
Oceania, excluding Australia and New Zealand	4	2.8	555	7
	1,541 (46.9%)		69,265 (51%)	

*Including Turkey

Source: United Nations Statistical Yearbook, 1965, Tables 2 and 19; United Nations Demographic Yearbook, 1965, Tables 1 and 3.

Table I-2

Indices of Economic Development

| Country | Per capita national income in dollars * | Per capita consumption, 1964 | |
		Energy in kgs. of coal or equivalent	Industrial steel in kgs.
United States	1964 : 2,700	8,772	615
United Kingdom	1964 : 1,365	5,079	438
West Germany	1964 : 1,415	4,230	579
France	1964 : 1,370	2,933	356
Italy	1964 : 760	1,659	221
Sweden	1964 : 2,025	4,320	623
Average**	1,605	4,500	470
U.S.S.R.	1964 : 890	3,430	355
East German Democratic Rep.	1964 : 1,205	5,569	424
Czechoslovakia	1964 : 1,685	5,789	498
Hungary	1964 : 1,445	2,824	224
Bulgaria	1964 : 650	2,410	124
Cuba	1964 : 575	931	29
Average**	1,075	3,490	275
Pakistan	1963 : 80	86	11
India	1963 : 80	161	16
Malaysia	1963 : 235	373	43
Thailand	1963 : 95	106	13
Iraq	1963 : 210	666	28
Average**	140	280	22
U.A.R.	1961 : 130	321	24
Morocco	1964 : 170	149	16
Zambia	1964 : 195	431	22
Nigeria	1962 : 90	38	6
Ghana	1964 : 250	120	11
Average**	165	210	16
Peru	1964 : 235	602	24
Argentina	1964 : 685	1,242	93
Brazil	1960 : 130	364	43
Chile	1964 : 445	1,078	74
Colombia	1963 : 230	494	31
Average**	345	755	53

*Figures calculated by the author from the data and conversion rates supplied by the United Nations Statistical Yearbook. For the socialist countries (excluding Cuba), the net material product at market prices has been used and the conversions have been made at the "base price."

**All averages are simple averages.

Source: United Nations Statistical Yearbook, 1965, various tables.

Table 1-3

Indices of Social Development

Country	Number of inhabitants per:				
	Doctor 1960-63	Teacher 1963-64	Registered pupil 1963-64	Books produced* 1964	Radio receiver 1962-64
United States	690	88	3.7	6,753	1.00
United Kingdom	840	135	5.8	2,077	3.39
West Germany	670	158	6.1	2,226	3.21
France	870	112	4.5	3,585	3.23
Italy	610	103	5.9	5,682	4.91
Sweden	960	93	5.4	1,161	2.60
Average	**775**	**115**	**5.2**	**3,580**	**3.05**
U.S.S.R.	510	118	4.4	2,910	3.15
East German Democratic Rep.	?	113	4.7	2,862	2.78
Czechslovakia	570	95	4.4	1,648	3.80
Hungary	650	110	5.1	2,108	4.05
Bulgaria	620	93	4.2	2,367	4.16
Cuba	1,200	141	4.7	14,120	
Average	**710**	**112**	**4.6**	**4,336**	**3.59**
Without Cuba	**(587)**			**(2,380)**	
Pakistan	7,000	383	11.3	65,000	183
India	5,800	?	8.3	35,920	110
Malaysia	10,500	144	5.3	18,280	20
Thailand	7,600	193	6.1	7,245	?
Iraq	4,800	164	6.2	24,170	10
Average	**7,140**	**121**	**7.4**	**30,120**	**81**
U.A.R.	2,500	215	7.0	10,870	13
Morocco	9,700	375**	11.0**	?	20
Zambia	8,900	?	9.5	?	300
Nigeria	34,000	509	17.4	213,700	94
Ghana	12,000	208	6.1	34,080	13.5
Average	**13,420**	**327**	**10.2**	**86,220**	**88**
Peru	2,200	149	4.9	11,900	5.5
Argentina	670	89	5.4	6,635	3.6
Brazil	2,700	170	7.0	14,910	10.5
Chile	1,800	?	4.9	5,380	5.4
Colombia	2,000	181	6.7	?	5.5
Average	**1,875**	**147**	**5.8**	**9,760**	**6.1**

*Production in number of titles.
**State education only.

Source: United Nations Statistical Year Book, 1965, various tables.

Table I-4

Gross Domestic Product at Factor Cost

	1958		1963		1965 (estimate)	
	Billions of $	%	Billions of $	%	Billions of $	%
Socialist countries (est.)	361	27.8	520	28.9	580	29
Developed capitalist countries	783	60.2	1,073	59.6	1,190	59.5
United States	413		540		590	
Third World	156	12.0	206	11.5	230	11.5
Latin America	52		68.5		77	
Southeast Asia and Oceania	61.5		79		86	
Middle East	11		15		17	
Africa	31.5		44.5		50	
World	1,300	100	1,800	100	2,000	100

Source: For the capitalist countries and the Third World in 1958 and 1963, figures were simply extracted from the Yearbook of the Statistics of National Accounts, 1965, Table 9B. For the socialist countries, the figures are estimates subject to a margin of error due a) to the fact that the "material net production" of these countries does not correspond in its components to the gross domestic product of the capitalist countries, and b) to the difficulty of evaluating the gross domestic product of China after 1958. The 1965 figures are estimates for all countries and are calculated from the 1963 figures increased by the relevant growth rates shown in various official documents.

Table I-5

**A. Index Numbers of Gross Domestic Product,
Excluding Services (1958=100)**

	Indices of total gross domestic product			Indices of per capita gross domestic product		
	1950	1965	Difference	1950	1965	Difference
World	68	146	**78**	78	128	**50**
U.S.S.R. and Eastern Europe	49	160	**111**	55	146	**91**
Developed countries, including South Africa	75	141	**66**	82	129	**47**
Of which:						
U.S.A./Canada	78	137	59	90	123	33
E.E.C.	65	144	79	70	133	63
E.F.T.A.	82	133	51	85	126	41
Developing countries	70	137	**67**	82	116	**34**
Of which:						
Latin America	67	139	72	83	114	31
South and East Asia	74	134	60	86	114	28

Source: United Nations Statistical Yearbook, 1966, Table 4.

**B. Annual Growth Rate of the Real Gross Domestic Product
at Factor Cost and Constant Prices (in %)**

	Total gross domestic product			Gross domestic product per capita		
	1950-60	1960-63	1960-64	1950-60	1960-63	1960-64
World	**5.3**		**4.9**	**3.5**		**3.0**
U.S.S.R. and Eastern Europe*	10.0		5.9	8.4		4.6
Developed countries	4.0		4.7	2.8		3.5
Developing countries	4.6	4.1	(4.3)	2.7	1.9	(2.1)

*Gross domestic product at market prices (constant prices), excluding services.

Source: Yearbook of the Statistics of National Accounts, 1965, Table 4B.

Chapter II

Agriculture and Fisheries

The Third World is a world of peasants. In almost every corner the population is engaged in agriculture. Table II-1 shows those engaged in agriculture as a percentage of the total population. Although these figures date from 1960, mobility between the different strata of the population in the Third World is so slow that they can be assumed to reflect the present situation pretty closely.

The predominance of agriculture as an occupation would suggest that agriculture must play a considerable, if not predominant, role in production. This is not the case. The indices given for separate countries in Part 2 show that the contribution of agriculture to the gross domestic product bears no relation to the proportion of the population engaged in agriculture. The averages range from 20 to 25 percent. The Third World thus makes a very disappointing contribution to the agricultural production of our planet. No figure could be found showing the percentage contribution made and it is hard to calculate it accurately. Table 8B of the *Yearbook of the Statistics of National Accounts, 1965* shows that in 1958 the total agriculture of the non-socialist world was divided as follows: Developed countries (including South Africa)—55.1 percent; developing countries—44.9 percent.

Taking 1958 = 100 as the base, the index of agricultural production in 1963 was 112 for the first group (but 116 in 1964) and 114 for the second group, and therefore it is reasonable to estimate that in 1963–64 the Third World (with South Africa taken back into it) contributed about 47 percent of the agricultural production of the non-socialist world.

15

But the real world includes the socialist countries. Calculations carried out on the basis of the total gross domestic product of each group of countries and the proportion contributed by agriculture point to the conclusion that in 1963–64 the share of the Third World in total agricultural production was only about 29 to 30 percent, with the balance fairly evenly divided between the socialist and the developed capitalist countries.

Here it must be emphasized that the Third World has almost half the world's inhabitants. Moreover, a greater proportion of its population is engaged in agriculture than in either of the other two groups (in spite of the fact that 65 percent of 700 million Chinese are rural) and it should, all things being equal, contribute about 60 percent of the world's agricultural production. The conclusion is that things are not equal—in other words, agricultural productivity in the Third World is poor. Part A of Table II-2 shows the wide variations in agricultural productivity between geographical regions in 1964–65. The table shows that, with the exception of cotton, Russian agricultural production was still much lower than that of the rest of Europe and North America. Most striking is the wide difference between the productivity of the developed agriculture of Europe and North America and that of South America, Asia, and Africa. Although the difference varies from crop to crop and South America is not so far behind, the difference for Africa and Asia is considerable: approximately 1:2 for rice, wheat, groundnuts (peanuts), potatoes; from 1:2.5 or 3 for maize, cotton, and barley; and from 1:4 or 5 for millet and sorghum.

Part B of Table II-2 gives something of an explanation for this poor agricultural production by showing that in 1964–65 the Third World used only the following proportions of total world consumption of fertilizers: nitrogenous fertilizers 17 percent, phosphate fertilizers 10 percent, and 7 percent of potash fertilizers. It might well be asked by what miracle the Third World, using such miserable amounts of fertilizer, managed to force its productivity to the level shown. A report issued early in 1967 by the Development Assistance Committee of the OECD estimates that by 1980 the underdeveloped countries will have to use five times the fertilizer they used in 1964–65 simply to maintain agricultural production at the level necessary to meet their own needs. This increase in the use of fertilizers will require the expenditure of $5 billion in foreign currency[1]—that is, some 50 to 60 percent of the aid actually going to the Third World.

Turning to animal husbandry, Table II-3 provides us with similarly useful comparisons. Surprise: in head of cattle, the Third World is at little disadvantage since in 1963–64 it raised 60 percent of the world's cattle, 52 percent of its sheep and goats, and 24 percent of its pigs (the low last percentage is attributable to large numbers of Moslems). But in spite of such large herds, in 1964 the Third World produced only 20 percent of the world meat supply, 23 percent of its milk, and, moreover, only 21 percent of the hens' eggs laid throughout the five continents. Finally, although having 52 percent of the world's sheep, the Third World contributed only 26 percent of world wool production. The level of productivity of animal husbandry thus seems to be as low as that of agriculture, if not lower. A closer look at the figures shows that in the field of animal husbandry, too, South America is definitely less badly off than is Africa or Asia—at least as far as meat production is concerned.

Agriculture and animal husbandry are backward and unproductive owing to a lack of technique and equipment and to an inadequate (social and economic) agrarian structure. But do the countries of the Third World have reserves of land which could provide a basis for expansion? The data shown in Table II-4 suggest that further clearing and extension of cultivation is possible. This is more a geographical and agronomic question than an economic one and should be left to others to resolve.

We have seen that the Third World plays a minor role in world production and is low in productivity. The question then arises: Has its agriculture at least begun to narrow the gap that separates it from the developed countries? Table II-5 provides the answers. Although Parts A and B relate to the same indices, they contain figures which differ somewhat because neither the bases used, nor the periods covered, coincide completely. Part B, ultimately the clearer demonstration, is slightly more discouraging than Part A: since it applies to a more recent period and takes a more recent

---

[1] *Le Monde*, April 22, 1967.

year as a base, it can be concluded that Third World agriculture was expanding more slowly from 1958 to 1964 than in earlier years.

However this may be, and even if the figures are not rigorously exact, it remains a fact that between 1958 and 1964 total agricultural production in the Third World increased more rapidly than in the United States and Canada but did not expand as much as in Western Europe. But during the same period per capita production remained stable in the United States and Canada and increased by 9 percent in Western Europe while it fell slightly for the Third World as a whole (from 100 to 98).

The above data applies to agriculture as a whole. Table II-5A distinguishes between the total and the share contributed by food production, showing where the rate of growth of per capita food production was about the same (Latin America and the Far East) as for the whole, or clearly slower (Africa and the Near East). On the other hand, the FAO study *The State of Food and Agriculture, 1965* points out that over the last ten years food production in the developed counties increased "at a much faster rate" than did non-edible agricultural production, while "a contrary trend was recorded for the developing countries."

In my view the most important distinction is between agricultural products for export and those intended for home consumption since some food products are entirely or principally for export. Table II-5C shows the increase in seven typical Third World export products between 1956 and 1964. These are commodities which are exclusively, or almost exclusively, produced by the Third World (with the exception of cotton) and consumed or used by the developed capitalist countries (except for bananas, since only one quarter of the total production is exported). Natural rubber has met with competition from synthetic rubber, but the other items all increased far more rapidly than the generality of Third World agricultural products. The simple average rate of growth of these products applied to the years 1958–64 is 31 percent—that is, 2.2 times greater than that of total agricultural production during the same period. This is evidence derived only by sampling major products but, however rough the results, they are clear enough to point to the conclusion that in present circumstances the principal motive force for the expansion of agricultural production in the Third World is demand from the developed capitalist countries. The United Nations *World Economic Survey, 1965 (Part II)* states that in Africa and western Asia "commercial agriculture developed very rapidly in some cases but by far the greater part of its production was composed of export crops."

It follows as a necessary complement to this that agricultural food production for local consumption is generally growing very slowly or not at all and is actually declining when taken per capita. This has led to increasing cries of alarm about hunger, malnutrition, and famine in the countries of the Third World. In 1966 Josué de Castro, former president of the FAO, addressed a conference organized by the National Union of Agricultural Grain Cooperatives. He "reminded his audience that at the present time one human being in three gets no more to eat than the deportees in the concentration camps and that the alleged laziness of the peoples of the poor nations is really the equivalent of the poor performance of a machine which is not given enough fuel."[2]

OECD experts calculate that the developing countries can at present only meet 93 percent of their caloric needs,[3] and Willard L. Thorp, president of the Development Assistance Committee of the OECD, wrote in *Development Assistance Efforts and Policies* (1966 Review) that there is "the possibility of a further serious decline in food availabilities per capita in the years to come" (page 77). He added that "much assistance given hitherto to agriculture has developed crops for export rather than food for local consumption" (page 79).

The FAO report quoted earlier[4] examines the problem of malnutrition in the Third World as it may develop in the coming decades:

By the end of the century the world's population should number between 5,300 and 6,800 million persons, the figure of 6 billion being the more probable. Almost 80 percent of this total will be

---

[2] *Le Monde*, May 19, 1966.
[3] *Le Monde*, July 22, 1966.
[4] *The State of Food and Agriculture, 1965.*

located in the developing countries which suffer from malnutrition
. . . The total quantity of foodstuffs available will have to increase
two-fold by the year 2000 merely to keep up with the expected
demographic growth without improving nutritional standards at all.
However, present nutritional levels in the developing countries are
so low that real needs are far greater than this. According to the
third FAO enquiry into world nutrition, 10 to 15 percent of the
world's population is undernourished and the proportion of human
beings suffering from hunger, malnutrition, or both is nearing 50
percent. The study suggests targets for overcoming malnutrition
which would require the underdeveloped countries to quadruple
their total food resources by the end of the century and multiply the
production of foods of animal origin by six (page 8, French edition).

Will these targets be reached? Mr. B. R. Sen, director general
of the FAO, seems to doubt it. At the second World Population
Congress in 1965 he stated: "The prospects are alarming. It is by
no means impossible that famine may break out in certain densely
populated areas within the next five to ten years."[5] The great
French specialist on these problems, René Dumont, foresees catastrophic famine in the Third World by about 1980.

It is doubtless true, as the 1966 OECD report put it, that "the
major responsibility for increasing food production must fall on
the less-developed countries."[6] Then, without appreciating its full
significance, the report adds a reference to the "self-reliance" of
the Chinese. The situation is such because the imperialist system
cannot be relied upon to reverse a situation which it created and
maintains, directly or through subservient governments, and which
serves its interests. We have seen that in the Third World the
production of foodstuffs destined for local consumption is stagnant or on the decline, while there is a constant increase in the
commodities destined for the markets of countries whose inhabitants can gorge themselves. The president of the Development
Assistance Committee has revealed that the aid from the rich to the
poor countries has usually served to develop the production of
commodities which will go to the surfeited rather than to increase

---

[5] *Le Monde,* September 14, 1965.
[6] OECD, *Development Assistance Efforts and Policies,* 1966 Review.

...d supplies for the hungry. And an article in *Le Monde* con-
...les:

> ...any case, when in official documents one refers to the transfer
> ...ood supplies to the Third World, one must never lose sight of
> ...omic reality: at present the OECD countries, Oceania, and
> ...Africa all import far more food from the underdeveloped
> ...es than they export to them (the difference is from 8 to 9
> ...rancs, excluding tea, cocoa, and coffee).[7]

...es
...re
...for
...for
...to
...eign
...the
...over-
...ch to
...World
...reased
...00,000
...er than
...tons to
...tes, and
...maritime
...his field,
...how im-
...—includ-
...ribution—
...n costs are

...II-6 to II-11 set out, by groups of countries and by
...ountries, the volume of production of those major
...commodities for which the Third World is either the
...rce, a dominant source, or a very important source.
...that the Third World produces all or nearly all of
...ply of coffee, cocoa beans, bananas, palm kernals,
...rubber; more than 70 percent of tea, groundnuts,
...uding that from conifers); nearly 60 percent of
...nt of cotton. The final destination of almost all
...s the markets and factories of the developed
...r rice and, to a certain degree, bananas). The
...s its belt and reaps for others.
...that production is often concentrated to a
...dia and Ceylon alone produce 68 percent
...ina and Nigeria 73 percent of its cocoa
...o-Kinshasa 50 percent of its palm nuts;
...cent of its jute; Malaysia and Indonesia
...(natural); India, Nigeria, and Senegal
...ts. This situation could well provide
...egy in the world markets, postulating
...anding and solidarity among these

...rld are bordered by some three-
...r planet and thus are in a nat-
...shing. Table II-12 shows that

Images écono-

in 1964 51 million tons of fish were caught, and that 20 million tons or 39.5 percent of this manna from the water was caught in the Third World. But this figure—the highest percentage noted, or to be found—must be interpreted in terms of Peru. In 1956 that country caught only 322,000 tons of ocean fish but by 1964 its catch had risen to the startling total of 9,130,000 tons (28 times as much) and it was maintaining the lead position in the world, reached two years earlier when it outdistanced Japan by some 3,000,000 tons.

The circumstances in Peru are peculiar. Its fantastic catch are composed mainly of *"anchovetas"* (small anchovies) which a very abundant in the Humboldt Current and can only be used fish meal. These *anchovetas* are certainly a source of wealth Peru, but their production is more akin to an industry than fishing and the ultra-modern techniques used by powerful for companies are more like extraction than fishing. Moreover, banks of *anchovetas* are said to be declining as a result of fishing and it would be prudent from now on to limit the ca 7 million tons per annum.[8] If Peru is omitted, the Third share of the 1964 world catch is only 22 percent and has inc less rapidly than that of the socialist countries (from 7,1 tons in 1956 to about 11,300,000 tons in 1964), but fast that of the developed capitalist countries (from 16,900,000 19,300,000 tons). The catches of Norway, the United St the United Kingdom are actually declining. In general, the nations of the Third World have made serious efforts in and when we look into the problems of nutrition, we se portant it is for them to continue and intensify this effor ing developments like freezing, canning, and better dis for fish is a food of high nutritive value and its producti lower than those of many others.

[8] According to Beaujeu-Garnier, Gamblin, and Delobez *miques du monde, 1966* (Paris: SEDES), p. 48.

Table II-1

**Agricultural Population as a Percentage
of Total Population in 1960**

Region	Percent
World	**52**
U.S.S.R.	35
Europe, except the U.S.S.R.	23
North America	8
South America	45
Asia, except China	64
China	65
Africa	70

Source: Food and Agricultural Organization Production Yearbook, 1965, Table 5B.

Table II-2

A. Agricultural Returns (1964-65)
(in quintals per hectare)

	U.S.S.R.	Europe (including People's Democs.)	North and Central America	South America	Asia	Africa
Rice (paddy)	24.3	46.5	32.2	15.3	18.3	17.8
Wheat	10.9	19.8	16.4	16.3	8.6	8.0
Barley	13.1	26.8	18.7	12.3	9.6	6.7
Maize	13.2*	25.1	30.7	13.6	11.5	10.8
Millet & Sorghum	9.9	20.0	24.0	11.6	5.0	c. 6.0
Potatoes	110	168	192	70	102	68
Cotton (lint)	7.3	4.1	6.0	2.0	1.9	2.6
Soybeans		15.0	15.4		7.1	
Groundnuts		16.7	15.7	12.9	8.9**	8.7

*1963-64
**Of which China=12.2.

Source: Food and Agricultural Organization Production Yearbook, 1965, Tables 13-70.

B. Consumption of Fertilizer (1964-65)
(in thousand metric tons)

	Nitrogenous fertilizers	Phosphate fertilizers	Potash fertilizers
Latin America	710	540	360
Near East	410	140	20
Far East, except Japan	1,280	470	255
Africa (1963-64)	200	220	180
Total for the Third World	2,600	1,370	815
Percent of world consumption	17%	10%	7%
World	**15,500**	**13,300**	**11,200**

Source: Food and Agricultural Organization Production Yearbook, 1965, Tables 109, 110, and 111.

Table II-3

Livestock

	Cattle 1963-64 (in millions of head)			Products 1964 (in thousand metric tons)		
	Cattle	Pigs	Sheep and goats	Meat	Milk	Hen eggs
Europe, including the People's Democracies	116.4	115.6	146.4	17,900	135,600	4,890
U.S.S.R.	85.4	40.9	139.6	7,400	63,100	c.1,450
U.S.A. and Canada	118.3	61.5	32.8	16,000	65,800	4,120
Latin America	211.9	88.4	170.3	7,300	23,600	1,040
Near East	33.2	0.1	176	1,300	12,700	290
Far East, excluding China	242.7	39.8	138.9	2,800	33,300	1,450
Africa	113.9	5.3	228.2	2,300	12,600	290 (1963)
Oceania	26.1	2.5	216.5	2,600	12,700	190 (1963)
World	992.3	534	1,364.7 (goats: 356)	67,300	359,600	14,500
Third World approximate %	60%	24%	52%	20%	23%	21%

Source: Food and Agricultural Organization Production Yearbook, 1965, Tables 76A, 76B, 77, 87A, 93, 99.

Table II-4

Land Utilization (1964)
(in millions of hectares)

	Total area	Agricultural area		Forested land	All other areas
		Arable land and land under permanent crops	Permanent meadows and pastures		
Europe	493	152	90	137	114
%	100	31%	18%	28%	23%
		49%			
North America (U.S.A., Canada, Greenland)	2,152 (Gr. : 218)	227	277	745	903
%	100	10%	13%	35%	42%
		23%			
Latin America	2,053	96	415	987	555
%	100	5%	20%	49%	26%
		25%			
Near East	993	85	86	128	694
%	100	9%	9%	13%	69%
		18%			
Far East	1,314	275	154	413	472
%	100	21%	12%	31%	36%
		33%			
Africa	2,496	248	603	659	986
%	100	10%	24%	26%	40%
		34%			

Source: Food and Agricultural Organization Production Yearbook, 1965, Table I.

Table II-5

A. Index Numbers of Agricultural Production by Region
(Average 1952-53 — 1956-57 = 100)

	All agricultural production				Food production			
	Total		Per capita		Total		Per capita	
	1952-1953	1964-1965	1952-1953	1964-1965	1952-1953	1964-1965	1952-1953	1964-1965
Western Europe	94	126	95	116	94	127	95	116
North America	99	116	103	98	99	118	103	100
Eastern Europe & the U.S.S.R.	89	144	92	125	90	146	93	127
Latin America	95	129	100	99	93	130	99	101
Far East, except China	91	129	95	104	91	129	94	104
Near East	94	136	99	106	93	131	98	102
Africa	94	128	98	99	94	124	99	96
All above regions	94	129	98	106	94	129	98	106

Source: Food and Agricultural Organization Production Yearbook, 1965, Tables 7 and 8.

B. Index Numbers of Agricultural Production in 1964
(1958 = 100)

	Production index for all agriculture		Per capita index	
Western Europe		116		109
U. S. and Canada		109		100
Latin America	110		93	
Far East, except China	115	simple	101	simple
Near East	115	average:	99	average:
Africa	117	114	100	98

Source: United Nations Statistical Yearbook, 1965, Tables 5 and 6.

C. Increase of Production in the Third World
Between 1956 and 1964

Coffee	+46%	Groundnuts	+43%
Tea	+28%	Cotton (lint)	+43%
Cocoa	+70%	Natural rubber	+18.5%
Bananas	+46%		

Source: Calculated by the author.

Table II-6

Production of Rice (Paddy) -- 1964-65
(in thousand metric tons)

World	**256,000**
U.S.S.R. and European socialist countries	600
China (est.)	81,000
Other Asian socialist countries	7,500
Total for socialist countries	**89,000**
United States	3,320
Western Europe	1,450
Japan	16,800
Australia	150
Total for developed capitalist countries	**21,700**
India	58,100
Pakistan	17,800
Thailand	9,600
Burma	8,200
South Vietnam	5,200
Philippines	4,000
U.A.R.	2,000
Madagascar	1,300
Total for Third World	**145,330**
Third World % of world total	57%
Third World % of world total except the socialist countries	87%

Source: Food and Agricultural Organization Production Yearbook,
1965, Table 21.

28

Table II-7

A. Tea Production in 1964
(in thousand metric tons)

World, except China and U.S.S.R.	870
(World, except China and U.S.S.R., in 1956)	(682)
(China, 1959)	(153)
(U.S.S.R., 1963)	(45)
Japan	83
India	372
Ceylon	218
Indonesia	45
Pakistan	28
Total for Third World	787
% of world total, except China and U.S.S.R.	90%
% of world total (approximate), including China and U.S.S.R.	72-73%

Source: United Nations Statistical Yearbook, 1965, Table 44.

B. Coffee Production in 1964
(in thousand metric tons)

Latin America	**1,830**
of which: Brazil	600
Colombia	486
Mexico	145
El Salvador	125
Africa	**1,030**
of which: Ivory Coast	202
Angola	192
Uganda	185
Asia	**250**
of which: Indonesia	132
World total	**3,160**
Third World total	**3,120**
(Third World total in 1956)	(2,260)

Source: United Nations Statistical Yearbook, 1965, Table 30.

Table II-8

A. Cocoa Bean Production in 1964
(in thousand metric tons)

Africa	**1,195**
of which: Ghana	580
Nigeria	298
Ivory Coast	147
Cameroons	94
Latin America	**305**
of which: Ecuador	50
Dominican Republic	40
Mexico	30
Asia and Oceania	**32**
World total = Total for the Third World	**1,530**
(World total = Total for the Third World in 1956)	(900)

Source: United Nations Statistical Yearbook, 1965, Table 29.

B. Banana Production in 1964-65
(in thousand metric tons)

World	**24,000**
Developed capitalist countries (Spain, Australia, etc.)	470
Latin America	16,130
Asia	6,160
Africa	1,200
Oceania	40
Total for the Third World	**23,530**
% world	98%
(Total Third World, average 1949-53)	(13,750)

Source: Food and Agricultural Organization Production Yearbook, 1965, Table 52.

Table II-9

A. Groundnut Production in 1964
(in thousand metric tons)

United States	1,000
Western Europe	20
Japan	130
Total developed capitalist countries	**1,150**
China	2,290
India	6,176
Indonesia	404
Burma	376
Total Third World in Asia	**7,250**
Nigeria	1,252
Senegal	1,000
Total Africa	**4,570**
Brazil	668
Argentina	439
Total Latin America	**1,300**
World, except U.S.S.R.	**16,700**
Third World	**13,120**
– % world, except U.S.S.R.	79%
= % world, except socialist countries	91%
(Total Third World in 1956)	(9,200)

Source: United Nations Statistical Yearbook, 1965, Table 33.

B. Palm Kernel Production in 1964
(in thousand metric tons)

Nigeria	407
Congo-Kinshasa	122
Sierra Leone	53
Dahomey	50
World total = Total for Third World except for negligible amounts	**1,060**
(Total for Third World except for negligable amounts in 1956)	(1,040)

Source: United Nations Statistical Yearbook, 1965, Table 39.

Table II-10

A. Cotton (Lint) Production in 1964
(in thousand metric tons)

United States	3,305
Western Europe	154
Total developed capitalist countries	**3,460**
U.S.S.R.	1,800
People's Democracies of Europe	25
Total socialist countries, except China	**1,825**
(China in 1959)	(2,410)
Brazil	580
Mexico	550
Total Latin America	**1,825**
India (1963)	980
Pakistan	380
Turkey	326
Total Third World in Asia	**2,180**
U.A.R.	504
Sudan	173
Total Africa	**1,020**
World	**11,900**
Third World	**5,025**
= % world	42%
= % world, except socialist countries	59%
(Third World total in 1956)	(3,520)

Source: United Nations Statistical Yearbook, 1965, Table 31.

B. Jute Production (1964-65)
(in thousand metric tons)

India	1,380
Pakistan	967
Thailand	248
World = Third World except for negligible quantities	**3,110**
(World average 1948-49 -- 1952-53)	(2,280)

Source: Food and Agricultural Organization Production Yearbook, 1965, Table 73.

Table II-II

A. Natural Rubber Production in 1964
(in thousand metric tons)

Malaysia	837
Indonesia	649
Thailand	222
Ceylon	112
World total = total for Third World	**2,275**
(World total in 1956)	(1,920)

Source: United Nations Statistical Yearbook, 1965, Table 49.

B. Roundwood Production in 1964 --
Excluding Resinous Conifers
(in millions of cubic meters)

United States	80
Japan (est.)	25
Western Europe	93
Australia, New Zealand	15
Total developed capitalist countries	**213**
U.S.S.R. (est.)	60
European socialist countries	48
Total	**108**
Africa	201
Latin America	317
Asia (Third World)	253
Total Third World	**771**
World (seemingly excepting China)	**1,003**
Third World % of total world (except China?)	77%

Source: United Nations Statistical Yearbook, 1965, Table 48.

Table II-12

Fish (Fresh Water and Ocean)
(in thousand metric tons live weight)

	1956	1964
U.S.S.R.	2,616	4,475
European socialist countries	c. 300	650
China	2,640	*
Other Asian socialist countries	c. 480	760
Cuba	16	36
Total socialist countries	c.6,050	11,860
U.S.A. and Canada	4,100	3,850
Norway	2,187	1,608
Spain	762	1,197
United Kingdom	1,050	975
Iceland	517	973
Denmark	463	871
France	624	780
Other European capitalist countries	2,347	2,606
Japan	4,773	6,335
Total developed capitalist countries (including Australia and New Zealand)	**16,910**	**19,330**
Peru	322	9,130
Chile	188	1,160
Other Latin American countries	555	1,270
Total Latin America	**1,065**	**11,560**
Southwest Africa	243	669
South Africa	293	586
Other African countries	1,364	1,655
Total Africa	**1,900**	**2,910**
India	1,012	1,320
Philippines	416	623
Thailand	218	577
Other Asian non-socialist countries, plus Oceania	2,829	3,420
Total Asia and Oceania (Third World)	**4,475**	**5,940**
Total Third World	**7,440**	**20,410**
World	**30,400**	**51,600**

*Catch estimated at at least six million tons on the basis of 5,800,000 tons for 1960 for all aquatic products.

Source: United Nations Statistical Yearbook, 1965, Table 50.

Chapter III

Minerals and Energy

It is well known that most of the countries of the Third World extract large quantities of products from the sub-soil, especially minerals and petroleum. But how does their production relate to that of the world and that of the two other groups of countries? Table III-1A does not give an exact answer, but it makes a first assessment possible. The note beneath the table shows that the "less industrialized" group of nations, as defined by the United Nations, is not identical with our Third World. It probably excludes a few South American countries—for instance, Venezuela —and, on the other hand, includes several southern European countries. It would be rash to assume that these differences balance out, especially as regards minerals (column 3); Table III-1B has therefore been added, giving indices of the growth of the extractive industries.

The first two groups in Table III-1B embrace almost all of what I have termed the developed capitalist countries. With the exception of coal, the average indices are very different from those in Table III-1A for 1965. Clearly the other two groups do not cover the Third World since Africa and the Middle East are missing. However, the known fact that there has been rapid development in Africa in this field and a comparison of these average indices with the earlier ones make it fair to say that between 1958 and 1965 there was greater expansion in the production of minerals in the Third World than in the advanced capitalist countries.

In his extremely well-documented work, Paul Bairoch goes further and disputes the index of production calculated by the

35

United Nations for the extractive industries:[1] "When we examined the data in this index and those related to total production for the underdeveloped non-Communist countries as a whole, it appeared that the index was biased." He became resigned to calculating an index himself, based on the combined production of the non-Communist underdeveloped countries. This index used the same base—1958 = 100—and for 1965 showed 178 for minerals, a much higher figure than that obtained for the advanced capitalist countries.

Knowing this, how does the Third World stand in relation to the rest of the world as far as the extractive industries and their component parts are concerned? A study of the imperfect data in Table III-1A, corrected as far as possible by those referred to above, leads us to the conclusion that in 1965 the Third World supplied some 27 to 28 percent of the world's production from the extractive industries, of which 6 to 6.5 percent was for coal, 26 to 28 percent was for minerals, and 42 percent was for petroleum and gas.

We should complete these general observations by looking at the figures for energy and its various sources (Table III-2). This gives us more precise and reliable figures for coal, petroleum, and gas since it refers to quantities produced in 1964–65. The table confirms that the Third World produces little coal—a source of energy on the decline—and little natural gas—a source in its early stages and one whose production pattern may soon change completely. Little electricity is produced, but this is usually only developed to meet the needs of industrialization. On the other hand, the Third World is already the dominant producer of petroleum. Table III-2 shows that although the socialist countries and the U.S.A. generally meet their own energy requirements, the other advanced capitalist countries meet their needs only by depending on the Third World (the Middle East and Latin America), which itself consumes only a little more than one-third of the total volume of energy it produces.

The Third World is still a modest producer of materials ex-

---

[1] Paul Bairoch, *Diagnostic de L'évolution économique du tiers-monde 1900–1966* (Paris: Gauthier-Villars Editeur, 1967), p. 70.

tracted from the sub-soil. Its real importance in this area relates less to the absolute volume of production than to the fact that—since almost all minerals are exported—mineral deposits are either important or decisive to the industries in the advanced capitalist countries.

In fact, the Third World is the principal—and often almost the only—source of many metal ores which modern industry utilizes in large quantities and in most cases this predominance is becoming increasingly greater. Tables III-3 to III-7 provide interesting data on this point.[2]

The Third World's share of iron ore production increased from 13 percent of a world total of 200 million tons in 1956 to 23 percent of 300 million tons in 1964. While the exploitation of new deposits in Canada and Sweden is anticipated, it was also expected that by 1966 Angola would produce some 5 million tons of high grade ore and that by 1968 Mauretania would produce 7.5 million tons, although neither of these countries figured as producers up to 1964.[3] This shows how the wind is filling the sails of the Third World in a key sector in which it had been a relatively late starter.

The Third World's share in world production of antimony remained at 50 to 52 percent, while the world total rose by 18 percent between 1956 and 1964. But over the same period its share of bauxite production increased from 57 percent to 59 percent while the total rose by about 60 percent. And Africa, which at present contributes only 6 percent to the total world bauxite production, holds about one-third of world reserves.[4]

Between 1956 and 1964 the world production of chrome ore was on the decline, but the Third World's contribution rose from 89 to 94 percent. World production of copper ore rose from 3.5 million tons in 1956 to more than 5 million tons in 1964 and the Third World's contribution rose from 42 to 44 percent. Over the same period, its share of manganese ore production rose from 42 to 45 percent while the world's total increased by one quarter. The production of cobalt ore remained stationary while the Third World's share rose from 69 to 72 percent.

---

[2] All the figures for minerals are given in metal content.
[3] According to Beaujeu-Garnier, *op. cit.*
[4] *Ibid.*

Outside of that produced by the socialist countries, almost the whole of the world's supply of tin concentrate (95 to 96 percent) is produced by Third World countries. The total rose sharply between 1956 and 1957, then fell, to recover by 1964. Only lead and zinc ore, often found in combination, show a darker picture: Third World production declined between 1956 and 1964 (respectively from 29 to 25 percent and from 24 to 21 or 22 percent). World lead production stagnated or increased slightly, but zinc advanced definitely from 1964 to 1965. The decline in the relative value of the Third World's production of both ores was largely due to a fall in the absolute value contributed by Mexico, the principal producer.

The Third World's contribution to the production of natural phosphates has also fallen (33.7 to 30.4 percent) but this is mainly due to the spectacular increase in Soviet extraction, which multiplied 2.5 times between 1956 and 1964. During the same period production of the main Third World producer, Morocco, did not quite double, while United States production rose to 46 percent of the world total, which itself increased from 34 to 57 million tons.

On the other hand, developments in crude oil production are very favorable to the Third World. Between 1956 and 1965 world production leapt from 840 to 1,500 million tons and the Third World's share increased from 42 to 52 percent. At the same time, Soviet production bounded from 84 to 224 million tons, while that of the United States climbed slowly from 354 to 377 million tons. It can be understood why that nation is so interested in the oil deposits of the underdeveloped countries, which, at the end of 1964, were absorbing 42 percent of all United States capital invested in the Third World.

To summarize, we can say that over the last ten years the Third World has made progress in the extractive industries generally—spectacularly so in crude oil and iron ore production; considerably in bauxite, copper, manganese, and natural phosphates; moderately in antimony and cobalt ore. On the other hand, production of tin concentrate and chrome ore has stagnated, and zinc and lead ore production has declined, possibly only relatively. Bairoch estimated that during the earlier years of the period 1957 to 1965 the evolution of Third World mineral production was irregular but that since 1962 there has been regular growth on the order of 10 percent per annum.[5] Analysis and computation of the development and prospects of the advanced capitalist countries in this field led him to observe "progressive exhaustion of the richest or most profitable deposits in the developed countries" and to record that "the Third World's share of production from extractive industries is growing." He adds: "This trend is liable to continue."

The United Nations *World Economic Survey*[6] notes concerning the industrialized countries: "If, in the case of many mineral products, an increasing proportion of national requirements have been met by imports, this is because they have grown more rapidly than local mineral production (much of which is coming up against the law of diminishing returns), and this in spite of the notable increases in production in some instances." Noting that the United States is a net exporter of most primary products, the document observes that it is "in general, only heavily dependent on imports of minerals."

This leads to the conclusion that the Third World's part in world production of extractive industries, already considerable, is likely to continue to grow, to the detriment of the advanced capitalist countries whose deposits are becoming exhausted or less productive. This advanced capitalist group of countries has consequently become more dependent on the mineral production of the Third World, and will become more so as time goes on, most especially for key products such as petroleum, iron ore, and bauxite. I shall return to this subject, which I consider to be one of the most vital elements in the structure of present and future economic relations between the two groups of countries.[7]

To conclude, what has already been recorded for several major agricultural products holds for a considerable part of mineral and allied production: not only does the Third World as such make a

---

[5] Bairoch, *op. cit.*

[6] *World Economic Survey, 1963*, p. 69.

[7] A United Nations statement, dated April 1967, records a proposal by Secretary General U Thant, that an inventory be drawn up of the resources of developing countries in minerals, hydrolics, and energy on a world scale. This inventory would be of outstanding interest but would take five years.

major contribution to total world production, but a very small number of countries together hold a privileged position. Thus, three countries in geographical proximity to each other—Surinam, Jamaica, and British Guiana—produce 43 percent of the world's bauxite (55 percent if the socialist countries are excluded). Three others—South Africa, Bolivia, and Mexico—produce 43 percent of the antimony ore extracted throughout the world (74 percent if the socialist countries are excluded). Chile, Zambia, and Congo-Kinshasa—the last two are neighbors—produce 34 percent of the world's total of copper ore (42 percent if the socialist countries are excluded). These same neighbors, Zambia and Congo-Kinshasa, alone produce 61 to 62 percent of the capitalist world's cobalt ore. The Third World as a whole is responsible for almost all the tin concentrate produced outside the socialist countries and Malaysia alone produces 41 percent. Adding the production of her neighbors Thailand and Indonesia, this proportion rises to more than 62 percent, and to 79 percent if Bolivia is included.

It is generally true that the contribution of the above-mentioned countries to the world market in the commodities concerned is greater than would appear from the production data. For instance, the two major and very large-scale producers of natural phosphates, the United States and the U.S.S.R., consume almost all they produce and so Morocco and Tunisia together may make only a small contribution to total world production and yet hold a preponderant position in international markets.

Table III-1

A. Index of Extractive Industries for the World, Excluding Asian Socialist Countries
(1958 = 100)

	Total	Selected extractive industries		
		Coal	Minerals	Crude petroleum and gas
U.S.S.R. and Eastern Europe				
% of world total in 1958	25.3	36.3	21.2	16.0
1965 Index	165	124	175	231
% of world total in 1965	28.5	41.3	25.6	21.3
Industrialized capitalist countries				
% of world total in 1958	55.9	58.7	54.8	53.6
1965 Index	120	97	138	123
% of world total in 1965	46.0	52.3	52.2	38.1
"Less industrialized" capitalist countries				
% of world total in 1958	18.8	5.0	24.0	30.4
1965 Index	198	139	134	231
% of world total In 1965	25.5	6.4	22.2	40.6

Note: The less industrialized countries are those for which in 1958 the increased value per capita added in the manufacturing industries was less than $125 (U.S.). It is possible, therefore, that they exclude some Third World countries and, on the other hand, include some countries which we would not classify as part of the Third World.

Source: Calculated from data in the United Nations Monthly Bulletin of Statistics, September 1966, November 1966, Special Tables A.

B. Indices for Mining for Some Groups of Countries in 1965
(1958 = 100)

	Total	Coal	Minerals	Crude petroleum and gas
U.S.A. and Canada	123	119	126	120
Europe, except socialist countries	108	90	118	225
Arithmetic average	115	105	122	172
Latin America	133	118 (1964)	127	138
East Asia and Southeast Asia, except Japan	190	185	165	199
Arithmetic average	161	152	146	168

Source: Extracted from United Nations Statistical Yearbook, 1966, Table 8.

41

Table III-2

Production and Consumption of Energy in 1964, and Overall Figures for 1965 (in million metric tons of coal or equivalent)

| | Production | | | | | Consump- |
	Total	Coal and lignite	Crude petroleum	Natural gas	Electr.	tion
United States and Canada	1,707	465	567	638	37	1,823
Western Europe	584	499	27	24	34	1,014
Japan	64	51	2*	3*	8*	161
Australia & New Zealand	38	36	0	0	2	56
Developed capitalist countries, 1964	2,393	1,051	596	665	81	3,054
1965	2,448	1,056	612	690	89	3,223
Socialist countries 1964	1,550	1,048	323	167	13	1,473
(of which: U.S.S.R.)	(870)					(781)
1965	1,628	1,069	350	195	14	1,543
Latin America	358	8	308	35	6	177
Middle East	568	6	557	5	1	53
Third World, extr.-Or.	128	79	39	6	4	136
Africa	97	49	45	1	1	71
Third World, 1964	1,151	141	949	47	12	437
1965	1,254	153	1,040	51	10	465
World, 1964	5,094	2,240	1,868	879	106	4,964
1965	5,330	2,278	2,002	936	113	5,231
% for the Third World, 1964	22%	6%	51%	5 %	11%	9 %
1965	23%	7%	52%	5.5%	9%	8.8%

*Estimate.

Source: United Nations Statistical Yearbook, 1965, Tables 14 and 142; United Nations Statistical Yearbook, 1966, Tables 11 and 142.

Table III-3

**World Production of Iron Ore
(Metal Content) in 1964
(in thousand metric tons)**

World	**304,000**
U.S.S.R.	84,600
European People's Democracies	3,900
China and North Korea (est.)	23,000
Socialist countries	**111,500**
United States	47,700
France	19,800
Canada	19,200
Sweden	16,200
United Kingdom	4,500
Developed capitalist countries	**123,000**
India	12,400
Brazil	10,200
Venezuela	10,000
Liberia	7,000
Chile	6,400
Peru	4,360
Malaysia	3,700
Third World	**69,500**
Third World % of world	23%
(Third World % of world in 1956)	(c. 13%)

Source: United Nations Statistical Yearbook, 1965, Table 56.

Table III-4

Various Extractive Industries — Production in 1964

COAL (in millions of metric tons)	
WORLD	**2,110**
United States	455
United Kingdom	197
West Germany	143
Developed capitalist countries	**985**
U.S.S.R.	409
Poland	117
China (est.)	400
Socialist countries	**985**
Third World	**140**
Third World % of world	6.5%

ANTIMONY ORE (metal content, in metric tons)	
WORLD	**64,000**
Developed capitalist countries	**4,200**
China	15,000
U.S.S.R.	6,100
Socialist countries	**26,800**
South Africa	12,900
Bolivia	9,600
Mexico	4,800
Third World	**33,000**
Third World % of world	51-52%
Third World % of world 1956	51-52%

BAUXITE (in thousand metric tons)	
WORLD	**34,200**
France	2,400
United States	2,000
Developed capitalist countries	**6,600**
U.S.S.R.	4,300
Hungary	1,500
Yugoslavia	1,300
China	400
Socialist countries	**7,500**
Jamaica	7,800
Surinam	4,000
Guinea	1,700
British Guiana (est.)	2,900
Third World	**20,100**
Third World % of world	59%
Third World % of world 1956	57%

CHROME ORE (metal content, in thousand metric tons)	
WORLD, except socialist countries	**1,115**
Third World	c. **1,050**
Third World % of world	94%
Third World % of world 1956	89%

Source: United Nations Statistical Yearbook, 1965, various tables.

Table III-5

Various Extractive Industries — Production in 1964

COPPER ORE (metal content, in thousand metric tons)	
WORLD	**5,025**
United States	1,130
Canada	450
Japan	105
Australia	103
Developed capitalist countries	**1,885**
U.S.S.R.	700
China	90
Yugoslavia	63
Socialist countries	**940**
Chile	797
Zambia	632
Congo-Kinshasa	277
Peru	174
Third World	**2,200**
Third World % of world	44%
Third World % of world 1956	42%

MANGANESE ORE (metal content, in thousand metric tons)	
WORLD	**6,900**
Japan	100
Developed capitalist countries	**190**
U.S.S.R.	3,200
China	300
Socialist countries	**3,625**
South Africa	600
Brazil	594
India	540
Gabon	474
Ghana	222
Congo-Kinshasa	164
Morocco	154
Third World	**3,085**
Third World % of world	45%
Third World % of world 1956	42%

COBALT ORE (metal content, in metric tons)	
WORLD, except socialist countries	**14,900**
Congo-Kinshasa	7,740
Morocco	1,550
Zambia	1,425
Third World	**c. 10,720**
(Note: approximate figures	= 72%)
(1956	69%)

Source: United Nations Statistical Yearbook, 1965, various tables.

Table III-6

Various Extractive Industries — Production in 1964

LEAD ORE (metal content, in thousand metric tons)	
WORLD	**2,550**
Australia	381
United States	260
Canada	187
Developed capitalist countries	**1,115**
U.S.S.R.	360
China (est.)	100
Bulgaria	101
Yugoslavia	102
Socialist countries	**795**
Mexico	175
Peru	147
South-West Africa	89
Morocco	76
Third World	**640**
Third World % of world	25%
Third World % of world 1956	29%

ZINC ORE (metal content, in thousand metric tons)	
WORLD	**4,050**
Canada	662
United States	522
Australia	350
Japan	216
West Germany	111
Italy	109
Spain	100
Developed capitalist countries	**2,265**
U.S.S.R.	410
Poland	151
China	100
North Korea	100
Socialist countries	**995**
Mexico	236
Peru	231
Congo-Kinshasa	105
Zambia	47
Morocco	46
Third World	**830**
Third World % of world	20-21%
Third World % of world 1956	24%

TUNGSTEN CONCENTRATES (metal content, in metric tons)	
WORLD	**36,230**
United States	5,030
Portugal	1,060
Australia	1,010
Developed capitalist countries	**8,765**
China (est.)	12,240
U.S.S.R. (est.)	6,600
North Korea (est.)	2,400
Socialist countries	**21,240**
South Korea	3,590
Bolivia	1,245
Third World	**6,225**
Third World % of world	17%

TIN CONCENTRATES (metal content, in metric tons)	
WORLD, except socialist countries	**149,500**
Developed capitalist countries	**7,270**
Malaysia	60,965
Bolivia	24,590
Indonesia	16,610
Thailand	15,845
Nigeria	8,860
Third World	**142,230**
Third World % of world except socialist countries	95%
in 1956	96%

Source: United Nations Statistical Yearbook, 1965, various tables.

Table III-7

Various Extractive Industries — Production in 1964

CRUDE PETROLEUM (in millions of metric tons)	
WORLD	**1,410**
(1965)	1,507
United States	377
Canada	37
Developed capitalist countries	**433**
U.S.S.R.	224
Romania	12
Socialist countries	**249**
Venezuela	178
Kuwait	107
Saudi Arabia	86
Iran	84
Iraq	62
Libya	42
Algeria	26
Third World	**728**
Third World % of world	51.6%
Third World % of world 1956	42%

NATURAL PHOSPHATES (in thousand metric tons)	
WORLD, except Asian socialist countries	**57,100**
United States	23,330
Developed capitalist countries	**26,650**
U.S.S.R. (est.)	13,000
Socialist countries, except in Asia	**13,100**
Morocco	10,100
Tunisia	2,750
Senegal	800
Togo	800
U.A.R.	610
Jordan	570
South Africa	580
Third World	**17,350**
Third World %, except the Asian socialist countries	30.4%
in 1956	33.7%

NATURAL GAS (in billions of cubic meters)	
WORLD, except Asian socialist countries	**652**
United States	440
Canada	39
Italy	8
France	5
Developed capitalist countries	**500**
U.S.S.R.	109
Romania	16
Socialist countries, except in Asia	**128**
Venezuela	6
Argentina	4
Indonesia	3
Third World	**24**
Third World % of world, except Asian socialist countries	4%

Source: United Nations Statistical Yearbook, 1965, various tables.

47

Chapter IV

Manufacturing

We will make one more attempt to determine the contribution of the Third World to total world production, in this case for the third and last category, production. Table IV-1 is derived from the same sources as the corresponding table for the extractive industries. It also has the disadvantage of including under the heading "Less industrialized capitalist countries" some which do not exactly fit with my Third World. However, the data which it gives for 1965 are comparable to those given for 1964 in Table 9 of the *United Nations Statistical Yearbook, 1965,* and this leads us to believe that Table IV-1 gives a very good approximation of reality.

On this basis it must be admitted that the manufacturing industries of the Third World represented only about 6.5 percent of world production in 1965—a little less than 10 percent for light industry and 5 percent for heavy industry, subject to what will be said below about these two categories. This is far below the figures of 29 to 30 percent for agriculture and 27 to 28 percent for the extractive industries, which will cause no surprise since it is universally known that underindustrialization is the worst of the many ills of the Third World.

Almost none of the mineral and agricultural raw materials produced by the Third World find their way to its factories. The Third World is the sole producer of natural rubber, yet in 1964 its industrial consumption of this commodity was only some 18 percent, and this percentage (see Table IV-2) is somewhat generously calculated. It is also strange that the principal industrial consumers of natural rubber in the Third World produce little or no latex: in 1964 the countries (Thailand, Malaysia, Indonesia) which produced this raw material on a large scale had no conversion industry.

The textile industry—especially cotton textiles—was one of the first which many Third World countries began to develop and it is here that we find that the Third World uses the highest proportion of its own raw materials. Even so, in 1964 the Third World produced 42 percent of the world cotton harvest (59 percent if the socialist countries are excluded), yet in that year industrial consumption was only 26 percent of the world total and 11 percent was used by India alone (see Table IV-3B). The industrialized countries are also major producers of raw cotton; India however processes slightly more raw cotton than she produces.

Because it is generally agreed that iron and steel form the basis of industrialization, a number of Third World countries have been, rightly or wrongly, determined to have their *own* iron and steel industry. This applies especially to the major Latin American nations, to India and South Korea in Asia, and to South Africa and Egypt in Africa (where, moreover, Morocco and Algeria are planning or establishing their own). Yet in 1964 the Third World as a whole contributed only 4 percent of the world's steel (Table IV-4) while extracting 23 percent of its iron ore. With the exception of Argentina, the main iron and steel producing countries of the Third World process their own ore, at least partially.

On the other hand, the Third World is very far behind in aluminum production (Table IV-4) since it produces 59 percent of the world's bauxite and only provides 3 percent of the world's production of primary aluminum, although this is a very elementary conversion process. As in the case of rubber, the major producers of the raw material do not participate in its processing. A similar situation is true for tin: the Third World provides 95 percent of the concentrate produced in the world (excluding the socialist countries) and has only an 8.6 percent (Table IV-5) share in total industrial consumption (excluding the U.S.S.R.). Again, in 1964 the world's largest producers of the raw material played only the most insignificant part in processing it—with the sole exception of Indonesia, which processed a small part of its own production. The major industrial consumers of tin in the Third World appear to depend on imported concentrates—entirely so in the case of India and mainly so in the case of Brazil.

In 1964 the Third World extracted 30.4 percent of the world's natural phosphates (excluding the socialist countries of Asia), but only contributed 6.5 percent of the world's production of super-phosphates (Table IV-4). The principal producers of raw phosphates process almost none into superphosphate and the major Third World producers of this processed fertilizer depend entirely (India) or partly (South Africa, Brazil) on imports of natural phosphates: the development of this industry in these countries has been determined by their agricultural needs.

Table IV-6 shows the main producers of crude petroleum and their activities as refiners. It shows that Venezuela refines about one-third of the oil spouting from its wells and the other four Third World countries refine an average of 14 percent.

Finally, Table IV-7 shows that the Third World contributes 16 percent of total world production of primary lead (against 25 percent of the ore) and 7 percent of primary zinc (against 20 to 21 percent of the ore). But it would be over-generous to consider the smelting of metals a real industry if it stopped at this stage. The same holds true for aluminum (see above). Such first fusion is a manufacturing process when it is an integral part of a process which goes much further, but is only an extension of the extractive industry when the ingots produced are exported because in such cases the object of the first fusion is not to initiate an industrial process but to reduce the cost of transporting the ore. This is the case in Third World countries where mining enterprises are almost always dependant on the monopolistic capital of the developed capitalist countries.

We have also noted above that for each of the raw materials considered, the main producers are not usually those Third World countries which first embark upon processing them industrially (natural rubber, tin, phosphates) and, on the other hand, those Third World countries which undertake the processing of Third World raw materials are often only modest producers of those same materials and depend entirely or almost entirely on imports to supply their plants. No absolute conclusion can be made from this observation, but it can at least be stated that under present conditions of characteristic imperialist exploitation of Third World raw materials, the fact that a Third World country possesses a given raw material does not necessarily lead to related industrial activity. This is the exact opposite of the pattern of industrialization which occurred in what are now the developed capitalist countries.

It must be pointed out here that some of the statistical classifications used in United Nations documents, appropriate when applied to industrialized countries, become irrelevant when applied to the Third World. For example, the inclusion of first fusion metals under the heading "heavy industry" seems questionable since we have questioned even its inclusion in manufacturing where the Third World is concerned. Similar doubts arise with regard to the category of metal work and, in addition, "paper and paper goods" are included under "heavy industry," which seems questionable for any country. It appears, therefore, that the position of the Third World in the field of heavy industry is overstated in Table IV-1 and in the data given at the beginning of this chapter, while for light industry the reverse holds true.

However this may be, Table IV-1 indicates that between 1958 and 1965 the output of all types of manufacturing industry increased by 93 percent in the U.S.S.R. and European socialist countries, by 59 percent in the industrialized capitalist countries, and by 69 percent in those countries which approximate our Third World. Thus over the last seven years the absolute value of the industrial growth of the Third World exceeded that of the developed capitalist countries by 17 percent. But this in turn was exceeded by 35 percent by the socialist countries, which explains why the Third World's share in world industrial production remained the same in 1965 as it had been in 1958. Real gains were made by the Third World in relation to the developed capitalist countries—still the most industrialized in the world—but these vanish when related to a population growth of 2.4 percent in the former and 1.2 percent in the latter, from which it appears that the per capita growth rate was 5 percent per year for the Third World and 5.1 percent for the developed capitalist countries. Without worrying about the decimal points, it is safe to say that the Third World is not making up for the backwardness of its industrial production. Table IV-8A shows that the Third World is also behind the other two groups of countries in the growth of labor productivity. The figures are for the productivity of labor in all industries (extractive, manufacturing, electricity, gas).

Industrial productivity in the Third World is thus seen to have grown by 35 percent less than in the industrialized capitalist countries and to be 45 percent below the growth rate of the socialist countries of Europe.

This gap clearly has its very negative aspects, but at this early stage it might be asked if even the least productivity is not relatively advantageous to the Third World because it is linked with a greater number of jobs for a given output. For example, Table IV-3 shows that in the textile industry the Third World uses a larger proportion of ordinary looms and the developed capitalist countries use more automatic looms. However beneficial such a situation may be to the Third World at a particular point in time, it would be very undesirable for it to continue in a perspective of rapid, diversified, and continuing industrialization. The best factory and the best industrial techniques are in the long run always those of today or tomorrow, not of yesterday.

Although all Third World countries are seriously underindustrialized, this does not apply uniformly and, going from Argentina to Mali or Upper Volta and looking at many other countries on the way, differences are considerable.

Table IV-8B shows how the Third World's share of world manufacturing (not forgetting that it is only 6.5 percent of the whole) was divided in 1965. These figures cannot be considered very accurate, but the disparities are so great in comparison with population figures that they provide admissable evidence. Thus it can be said that Latin America is four times less underindustrialized per head of population than Africa and the Middle East and six times less so than Asia. And great differences exist between countries within the same continent. Some idea of this can be gained from Table IV-8C, which sets out the contribution of manufacturing to the gross domestic product in 1964 for a number of underdeveloped countries.

Table IV-1

Index of World Manufacturing Industries, Excluding Asian Socialist Countries
(1958 = 100)

	Total	Categories	
		Light industry	Heavy manufacturing
U.S.S.R. and Eastern Europe			
% of world total in 1958	27.8	28.3	27.5
1965 Index	193	153	220
% of world total in 1965	31.7	29.8	32.7
Industrialized capitalist countries			
% of world total in 1958	65.8	62.4	68.0
1965 Index	159	141	170
% of world total in 1965	61.9	60.5	62.5
"Less industrialized" capitalist countries			
% of world total in 1958	6.4	9.3	4.5
1965 Index	169	151	194
% of world total in 1965	6.4	9.7	4.8

Source: United Nations Monthly Bulletin of Statistics, September 1966, November 1966, Special Tables A. See Note to Table III-1A.

Table IV-2

Industrial Consumption of Natural Rubber in 1964
(in thousand metric tons)

World, except socialist countries	**1,950**
United States	490
Japan	206
United Kingdom	182
West Germany	152
France	127
Other recorded countries (6 countries)	224
Total for the recorded developed capitalist countries	**1,384**
India	60
Brazil	33
Other recorded countries (2 countries)	59
Total for recorded Third World countries	**152**
Non-recorded countries, included in world total	414

If the arbitrary assumption is made that the consumption of countries not detailed is divided equally between the advanced capitalist countries (Finland, Denmark, Norway, Ireland, Switzerland, Austria, Portugal, Spain, Greece, Israel, New Zealand) and the Third World countries, the consumption of each group of countries becomes:

Developed capitalist countries	1,591 = 82%
Third World	359 = 18%

Source: United Nations Statistical Yearbook, 1965, Table 169.

Table IV-3

A. Number of Cotton Looms Installed in 1964
(units)

	Ordinary looms	Automatic looms
World	**1,315,560**	**1,407,760**
U.S.S.R.	112,000	163,000
China	200,000	120,000
Other socialist countries	113,000	77,000
Total socialist countries	**425,000**	**360,000**
United States	0	288,360
Japan	297,390	88,090
Italy	11,540	73,820
United Kingdom	82,000	48,000
France	28,440	62,872
Total developed capitalist countries	**547,500**	**780,000**
India	180,940	24,530
Brazil	65,000	32,000
Mexico	14,000	30,500
Pakistan	12,600	22,000
Total Third World	**343,000**	**267,800**
Third World % of world	26%	19%

Source: United Nations Statistical Yearbook, 1965, Table 97.

B. Industrial Consumption of Cotton in 1964
(in thousand metric tons)

World	**10,830**	U.S.S.R.	1,485
		China	1,345
United States	2,000	Other socialist countries	700
Japan	735	**Socialist countries**	**3,530**
West Germany	285		
France	260	India	1,200
United Kingdom	235	Pakistan	285
Others	965	Brazil	260
Developed capitalist countries	**4,480**	Other Third World countries	1,075
		Third World	**2,820**
		Third World % of world	26%

Source: United Nations Statistical Yearbook, 1965, Table 167.

Table IV-4

Various Industrial Products
(in thousand metric tons)

STEEL PRODUCTION (1964)	
WORLD	**433,700**
U.S.S.R.	85,030
China (est.)	9,500
Other socialist countries	30,030
Socialist countries	**124,570**
United States	115,280
Japan	39,800
West Germany	37,370
United Kingdom	26,650
France	19,780
Developed capitalist countries	**290,960**
India	6,030
South Africa	3,110
Brazil	3,030
Mexico	2,280
Argentina	1,270
Other Third World countries	2,450
Third World	**18,170**
Third World % of world	4%

SUPERPHOSPHATE PRODUCTION (1963)	
WORLD, except Asian socialist countries, Canada, and several small countries	**42,500**
United States	11,790
Australia	2,910
Spain	1,810
Developed capitalist countries	**27,520**
U.S.S.R.	7,860
Other European socialist countries	4,380
European socialist countries	**12,240**
South Africa	850
India	580
Brazil	310
Third World	**2,740**
Third World % of world	6.5%

PRIMARY ALUMINUM PRODUCTION (1964)	
WORLD	**6,180**
U.S.S.R. (estimate)	1,000
Other socialist countries	390
Socialist countries	**1,390**
United States	2,320
Canada	760
France	320
Japan	270
Developed capitalist countries	**4,620**
India	55
Cameroons	50
Other Third World countries	65
Third World	**170**
Third World % of world	3%

Source: United Nations Statistical Yearbook, 1965, various tables.

Table IV-5

Industrial Consumption of Tin in 1964
(in metric tons)

World, except U.S.S.R., North Vietnam, North Korea	**179,540**
China	7,300
Poland	1,900
Czechoslovakia	1,800
East Germany	1,500
Yugoslavia	1,630
Other socialist countries (Cuba, Bulgaria, Hungary, Rumania)	960
Total socialist countries (except U.S.S.R., North Vietnam, North Korea)	**15,090**
United States	59,415
United Kingdom	19,145
Japan	18,235
West Germany	12,595
France	11,200
Other developed capitalist countries	28,440
Total developed capitalist countries	**149,030**
India	4,960
Brazil	2,030
South Africa	1,470
Indonesia	1,020
Other Third World countries	5,940
Total Third World	**15,420**
% Third World	**8.6%**

Source: United Nations Statistical Yearbook, 1965, Table 171.

Table IV-6

Petroleum Production in 1964
(in thousand metric tons)

	Crude petroleum	All petroleum products
Venezuela	178,230	59,004
Kuwait	106,719	11,731
Saudi Arabia	85,798	14,466
Iran	84,006	19,115
Iraq	61,626	2,585
(United States)	376,609	435,151

Source: United Nations Statistical Yearbook, 1965 Tables 75 and 124.

Table IV-7

Various Industrial Products in 1964
(in thousand metric tons)

PRIMARY LEAD		PRIMARY ZINC	
WORLD	**2,610**	**WORLD**	**3,710**
China (est.)	100	U.S.S.R. (est.)	460
U.S.S.R.	360	China (est.)	90
Other socialist countries	330	Poland	190
Socialist countries	**790**	Other socialist countries	215
United States	420	**Socialist countries**	**925**
Australia	210	United States	870
Canada	140	Japan	310
West Germany	110	Canada	310
Japan	100	Other developed capitalist countries	1,035
France	90	**Developed capitalist countries**	**2,525**
Other developed capitalist countries	340	Peru	70
Developed capitalist countries	**1,410**	Mexico	60
Mexico	160	Congo-Kinshasa	60
Peru	90	Zambia	50
South-West Africa	50	Other Third World countries	20
Other Third World countries	110	**Third World**	**260**
Third World	**410**	Third World % of world 7%	
Third World % of world 16%			

Source: United Nations Statistical Yearbook, 1965, Tables 132 and 135.

Table IV-8

A. Indices of Labor Productivity in Industry
(1958 = 100)

U.S.S.R. and Eastern Europe	1963	134
	1964	140
Industrialized capitalist countries	1963	127
	1964	135
"Less industrialized" capitalist countries	1963	119
Industrial manufacturing only	1963	117

Source: United Nations Statistical Yearbook, 1965, Tables 12 and 13.

B. Distribution of Manufacturing Industries
Among Regions of the Third World in 1965

Latin America	50%	per approx. 235 million inhab.
Southeast Asia	30%	per approx. 900 million inhab.
Africa and Middle East	20%	per approx. 400 million inhab.

Source: Figures calculated by the author.

C. Contribution of Manufacturing Industry to Gross
Domestic Product in 1964

Argentina	33%	Ceylon	6%
Mexico	28%	Malaysia (1963)	11%
Chile	19%		
Peru	20%	South Africa (1963)	28%*
Guatemala	14%		
Bolivia	15%	Morocco	14%
British Guiana	12%	Malawi (1963)	6%
Honduras (1963)	13%	Rhodesia	17%
		Tanzania	4%
Philippines	19%	Tunisia	15%
Burma	15%	Turkey	15%
Pakistan (1963)	11%	Zambia	6%
Thailand (1963)	12%	U.A.R. (1961)	17%
South Vietnam	11%	Jordan (1963)	8%
Cambodia	9%	Togo (1963)	5%

Note: For purposes of comparison, let us cite: West Germany: 41 percent; United Kingdom: 36 percent; France: 36 percent; United States: 30 percent.

*Including construction.

Source: United Nations Statistical Yearbook, 1965, Table 182.

Chapter V

Trade and Shipping

International trade offers the best background against which to display the size and nature of the production and trade relations between the countries of the Third World and the developed capitalist countries, and makes it possible to illuminate the bonds of reciprocal dependence to which it gives rise. It deserves, therefore, a more detailed examination and will be discussed under six headings:

1. Overall Development of Trade
2. Trading Partners
3. Composition of Trade
4. Terms of Trade
5. Maritime Shipping
6. Summary and Critical Analysis

1. Overall Development of Trade

Table V–1 analyzes world exports in 1965 by groups and subgroups of countries and by origin and destination. For comparative purposes—but by large groups of countries only—it also gives corresponding data for 1948 and 1956. The imperfections remarked upon in the notes are not serious. The fact that South Africa and Cuba are not grouped as in this book (cf. Chapter 1) does not affect the partial totals very much. The disparity between some of the totals and their components is reduced to minor significance by the method used to calculate percentages. And since, as in previous chapters, the argument depends on percentages, discrepancies will be taken into account only when they are big enough to conceal minor errors.

In 1965 the Third World's exports, valued at $36.7 billion, amounted to barely 20 percent of the world total, compared with 11 to 12 percent for the socialist countries and 68 to 69 percent for the developed capitalist countries. In 1956 the figures were 24 percent, 10 percent, and 66 percent respectively and in 1948, 30 percent, 6.5 percent, and 63.5 percent. Thus between 1948 and 1965 the Third World's share in world exports fell from 30 percent to 20 percent while that of the socialist countries grew from 6.5 percent to 11 to 12 percent and that of the developed capitalist countries from 63.5 percent to 68 to 69 percent. For the present, these figures should merely be noted, as it would be premature to draw conclusions before reaching the final section of the present chapter—that is, before taking into account the material presented in sections 3 and 4.

Returning to 1965, the total exports originating in the Third World were divided as follows: 32 percent from Latin America (235 million inhabitants); 23 percent from Africa (310 million inhabitants); 18.5 percent from the Middle East (70 million inhabitants), and 26.5 percent from South and East Asia (920 million inhabitants). In per capita terms, the Middle East is thus well in the lead because of its huge exports of crude oil. Latin America comes next, well ahead of Africa, while South and East Asia appear in this respect to be by far the most poverty-stricken parts of the Third World.

Table V–2A shows the share of various Third World regions in the Third World's gross domestic product and in its exports in 1965. The percentages for Latin America and Africa are of the same order, that for the Middle East is markedly different for the reason noted above, and the percentage is equally different in the opposite sense for South and East Asia. The latter appear to be so very underdeveloped that even opportunities for imperialist pillage are relatively poorer than elsewhere. It is widely believed that external trade is a far greater proportion of gross domestic product or gross national product in the underdeveloped countries than in the developed capitalist countries. It is true that in 1965 the exports of the Third World reached 16 percent of its total gross domestic product for the same year, against 10.75 percent for the developed capitalist countries, but in 1958 the respective figures were 15.8 percent and 9 percent. The first percentage rose scarcely at all and the second considerably more, suggesting that this particular gap between the two groups of countries is tending to decrease for reasons which will appear later (divergent changes in the terms of trade, artificially rapid growth of the trade of the industrialized countries), and it is probable that this decrease will continue. Many writers have tried to establish this divergence as a specific characteristic of development and underdevelopment, but, though it does exist between groups of countries, even if less and less, it seems much less significant when particular countries, whether from the same or different groups, are compared. Table V–3 demonstrates the fragility of over-generalized and pseudo-scientific conclusions drawn from the relationship between figures for external trade and gross domestic product or gross national product. Other factors than development and underdevelopment come into play, although it is not our purpose to analyze these here.

Returning to Table V–1, it will be more interesting to try to establish the extent to which the three large groups trade within and between themselves. In 1965, 73 percent of the Third World's exports went to the developed capitalist countries, 6 percent to the socialist countries, and 21 percent to other Third World countries (internal trade of the group). Twenty-one percent of exports from the capitalist countries go to the Third World, 4 percent to the socialist countries, and 75 percent to other developed capitalist countries (internal trade). As for the socialist countries, their internal trade absorbs 65 percent of their exports while 21.5 percent go to the developed capitalist countries and 13.5 percent to the Third World.

This leads to a first conclusion: Internal trade is predominant within both the developed capitalist countries (75 percent of all exports) and the socialist group (65 percent); the reverse is true for Third World countries, which exchange only 21 percent of their total exports among themselves. Thus while each of the first two groups is largely self-supporting in its external trade, this is not so for the Third World, which depends on the developed capitalist countries to take almost three-quarters of its exports.

Although the socialist countries have doubled the value of their imports from the Third World since 1948 and increased their exports somewhat less rapidly, they remained in 1965 such a minor trading partner (6 percent of the total)—in spite of China's increasing share—that no further attention will be paid to their trade.

Great attention must, however, be paid to trade between the developed capitalist countries and the Third World. In 1965 the total volume stood at $26.4 to $26.5 billion and was really the determining factor not only for the Third World as a whole but for each major region within it, since exports to the developed capitalist countries absorb the following percentages of total exports:

72 percent for Latin America
82 percent for Africa
76.5 percent for the Middle East
61 percent for South and East Asia

On the other hand, this same trade absorbs only the following percentages of the total exports of the advanced capitalist countries:

26.5 percent for the United States and Canada
16.5 percent for Western Europe
43 percent for Japan

It is worth repeating that in 1965 the dependence of each of the large groups of countries on their trade with the other was 73 percent for the Third World and 21 percent for the developed capitalist countries, while in 1948 the figures were respectively 68 percent and 31 percent. Thus the Third World is growing more and more dependent on the developed capitalist countries, which depend less and less on the Third World. On the basis of the 1965 figures this hypothetical argument can be made: If the developed capitalist countries brutally cut their trade with the Third World in half, their total trade would only be affected by some 10 percent while that of the Third World would collapse to 63 to 64 percent of its present level. Of course the hypothesis is absurd, but it simply serves to bring into sharp relief the present relative inequality which is characteristic of trade, however roughly balanced, between the two groups.

From this data and this trend many writers draw hasty conclusions which will be analyzed and refuted in the final section of this chapter. It seems desirable to lay special stress upon the figures underlying their arguments: These provide an inadequate foundation because they are limited to the quantitative-value aspect of the problem. This produces poor results unless account is taken of the essential quantitative volume and above all of the qualitative aspects, which we will discuss later.

To conclude a review of the trade of the Third World, Table V–4 presents data on the balance of trade of the major regions of the Third World. The region as a whole has a small trade deficit, rather smaller in 1965 than in 1956—but this is almost entirely due to the oil-exporting countries. If Venezuela were excluded, Latin America would have a small adverse balance instead of a favorable one. If Venezuela and the oil producers of the Middle East were excluded, the Third World would have a large adverse balance instead of a small one. Africa seems to be the region which has made the most progress since 1956, wiping out the greater part of its unfavorable balance of trade by developing several exports, notably minerals. As in other fields, South and East Asia are again the poorest of the poor. Their large adverse balance of trade in 1956 had more than doubled in absolute value by 1965; the extent to which the region's imports covered its exports fell from 83 to 75 percent.

2. Trading Partners

So far we have compared trade relations between the Third World and the developed capitalist countries. But within the overall movements between the two groups there are component trends which it is most instructive to study, taking the years 1956 and 1965. These are shown in Table V–5A.

Looking at the exports of the principle countries or groups of developed capitalist countries to the different parts of the Third World, it becomes apparent that:

1. The United States (responsible for more than nine-tenths of the United States/Canada total) sells mainly to Latin America, with a considerable amount to South and East Asia and relatively

little to the Middle East or Africa. One thing is most striking: Sales to Latin America dropped from 58 percent of the Third World total in 1956 to 47 percent in 1965 while, over the same period, sales to South and East Asia rose from 23 to 33.5 percent. Thus there has been a considerable transfer of exports from the most favored South American continent to the Asian continent where the United States seems to be eroding certain British trading positions.

2. Western Europe's export trade is better distributed over the four major zones of the Third World, although Africa clearly occupies first place. But here too the export trade of the most favored continent has declined from 41 percent of the total in 1956 to 37 percent in 1965 while the proportion of exports destined for Latin America (from 20 to 22 percent) and the Middle East (from 14 to 17 percent) increased. However, South and East Asia's share declined by 1 percent.

3. Japan's total exports, which fall far short of those of the above countries and are strongly oriented to South and East Asia, rose from 57 percent in 1956 to 61.5 percent in 1965. On the other hand, its exports to Africa fell from 25 percent to 19 percent over the same period.

To summarize, each of the three groups of advanced capitalist countries considered directs its exports principally to one of the three continents of the Third World: the United States to Latin America, Western Europe to Africa, Japan to Asia. But the United States' hold over Latin America is weakening, chiefly to the benefit of Western Europe. Western Europe's hold on African markets is likewise weakening but there does not seem to be any particular beneficiary, simply because the exports from the advanced capitalist countries to Africa are in general developing less rapidly than they are to the other regions of the Third World. Japanese exports to South and East Asia are still too small in absolute value to speak of a Japanese hold. Western Europe, which in 1956 had a clearly dominant position in regard to the absolute value of its exports to South and East Asia, is now being overtaken by the United States and seriously challenged by Japan—which has the most rapid rate of development.

If we now turn to the other side of the coin—the exports from various parts of the Third World to the principal developed capitalist countries or groups of countries—the following appears:

1. Latin America still exports primarily to the United States and Canada, closely followed by Western Europe, but the share of the former fell from 57 percent in 1956 to 47.5 percent in 1965, while that of Europe rose from 38 to 45.5 percent. The positions and trends are almost symmetrical with those recorded for the exports of the developed capitalist countries to Latin America.

2. Africa disposes of almost all it sells to Western Europe, whose share of African exports rose from 83 percent in 1956 to 85 percent in 1965. Here, however, symmetry is only relative: though Africa is at the top of the list of Third World regions receiving European exports, it only took 37 percent in 1965. This was four points lower than the 1956 figure—the opposite trend to that for Latin America.

3. The chief customer of South and East Asia is Western Europe, though its share of that region's exports fell from 51 percent in 1956 to 40.5 percent in 1965 while that of the United States and Canada rose from 27 percent to 31 percent and that of Japan from 15 percent to 21 percent. Here, as with Latin America, there is and continues to be a considerable degree of symmetry in the proportion of exports from the developed capitalist countries to South and East Asia and their imports from that region.

5. The geographical distribution of exports from the Middle East is less significant since they are preponderantly oil and go primarily to those countries which are the buyers and the nearest buyers.

We will now attempt to seek any broad conclusions which follow from this analysis of the state and trends of trade relations between the major components of the Third World and the group of developed capitalist countries. Although the data are somewhat complex, two dominant ideas emerge:

1. The countries or groups of countries of the Third World still trade mainly with the one or several developed capitalist countries of which they were formerly colonies, semi-colonies, or dependencies: Latin America with the United States; Africa with Western Europe and, more especially with Britain or France as the

case may be; South and East Asia with Western Europe also, and
especially with Great Britain.

2. However, there is an increasing tendency for these bilateral
trade links to weaken. If Africa appears to be an exception, this is
because we have been considering trade between groups of countries and in this case the weakening of predominantly bilateral
links has been to the benefit of other countries in the same group:
certain former French colonies trade less with France but rather
more with West Germany, Italy, or the Benelux countries, etc., and
vice versa. Although this dispersal was already underway, the
association of eighteen African countries with the European
Common Market has accelerated it.

It can, therefore, be said very generally that special preserves
are on the decline, even though they continue in individual cases
and resist strongly: networks of relationships are gradually but
increasingly replacing earlier channels—from a particular African
country to France, from Latin America to the United States, and
vice versa. It has already been seen, and will become increasingly
clear in subsequent sections, that these trade channels have not
changed their original character and illustrate the pillage of the
Third World within the framework of an international division of
labor which perpetuates the imperialist system and tends to
aggravate it. There may be no essential difference between colonialism and neo-colonialism, but it is interesting to note that the
latter may operate through different channels. Multilateral trade
progressively tends to replace the almost grotesquely restricted
bilateral trade of fifteen to twenty years ago. The exploiter of any
particular Third World country no longer has the face of any
individual European or North American country, but is the
face of imperialism itself.[1]

---

[1] On the other hand, Mr. Raúl Prebisch, the secretary-general of the
United Nations Conference for Trade and Development, speaking especially about the association of the eighteen African states with the EEC
and the plans for an inter-American common market, warned against the
danger of a "vertical division" of the world which would tie Africa more
closely to Europe and Latin America more closely to the United States.

But for the moment the figures show the reverse, and it is this that we
have been talking about. A report issued by the Board of Trade on the
basis of early 1967 figures shows that the Commonwealth countries are

3. Composition of Trade

Table V-6A analyzes, for 1965, the exports and imports of the developed capitalist countries and of the Third World, dividing them by categories of goods and in many cases giving the 1956 figures for reference.

It appears that in 1965 17.5 percent of Third World exports to all destinations consisted of manufactured goods and 82.5 percent consisted of fuels (almost all oil), raw materials, and foodstuffs. These two percentages become 16.2 and 83.8 if only those Third World exports destined for the advanced capitalist countries are considered. But two reservations must be taken into account:

1. We saw in the preceding chapter that in the United Nations classification, first fusion metals are included under manufactured goods—and, what is more, under the heading "heavy industry." In this case also, including these raw materials as manufactured goods unduly inflates their volume and reduces that of the raw materials with which they should be classified. Although they are the product of an elementary transformation process, they are no more than a raw material since they cannot be used as they are. The United Nations *World Economic Survey* for 1962, Part I, figures the contribution of common metals to the exports of the developing counties at 4.5 percent of the 1959 total. Given the growth of the export of primary metals, it seems reasonable to estimate it at 6 percent in 1965 and 4 percent in 1956.

Table V-6B, calculated on this basis, shows that real manufactured goods made up 11 percent of the Third World's exports in 1965 (10 percent of those destined for the developed capitalist countries), and foodstuffs, fuels, and raw materials made up 88 to 89 percent (90 percent of that destined for the developed capitalist countries).

2. Paul Bairoch[2] points out correctly that including Hong Kong as one of the countries classified as "less developed" by the United Nations and as the Third World by us distorts the figures

---

developing their trade with third parties more rapidly than with Great Britain. (*Le Monde,* August 19, 1967.)

[2] Bairoch, *op. cit.*

for Third World exports of manufactured goods. He states that since more than 75 percent of Hong Kong's exports consist of manufactured goods, this territory, which provides only 3 percent of the Third World's exports, contributes about 16 percent of its exports of manufactured goods. It would thus be justifiable to reduce the proportion of industrial goods in the exports of the Third World by some 1.6 percent.

But this is not a field in which measurements can be refined to the last decimal point, and it is wiser to observe that by and large some 90 percent of exports from Third World countries consist of raw or semi-raw materials which fall into three major categories—foodstuffs, combustible minerals (oil), and raw materials—and, on the other hand, only 10 percent of Third World exports consist of manufactured goods. It is clear that this distribution is not exactly the same for each of the major regions of the Third World and that the proportion of manufactured products would be higher for Latin America and lower for Africa, but data are not available to evaluate such differences precisely.

However this may be, the analysis of trade between the Third World countries and the developed capitalist countries provides a startlingly characteristic picture of the international division of labor. Ninety percent of the sales by the first group to the second consists of raw or semi-raw materials while 79 percent of exports in the other direction consists of manufactured goods. The complementary specialization of the two groups is almost complete.

Even more serious for many Third World countries is the fact that over-specialization is even greater than can be seen from general statistics. Table V-7A shows how agricultural exports, often of only one or two products, compose the bulk of the exports for some Latin American and African countries. Thus a single product provides 50 percent of exports for the United Arab Republic and Syria (cotton), 72 percent for Colombia (coffee), and 84 percent for Réunion (sugar). Table V-7B shows other examples, including minerals.

Paul Bairoch puts it this way: "For the Third World in general in 1963, 55 percent of exports were composed of products which are dominant in one country; for the developed countries this proportion is only 18.5 percent."[3] He goes on to insist on the need for the diversification of the external trade of the countries of the Third World while conceding that this "is obviously largely dependent on their industrialization."

Is the progress in the industrialization of the Third World over the last ten years—real in absolute value though small or nil in relative terms (see Chapter 4)—reflected in the composition of exports? It was in the hope of tracing an advance that figures for 1956 were noted under many of those for 1965 in Table V-6A. But these figures are heavily distorted by the growth in sales of oil, much more rapid than that of other products. From 1956 to 1964 the Third World's production of oil almost doubled in volume (and it is practically all exported), while from 1956 to 1965 its total exports grew by slightly less than 50 percent in current value (Table V-1). The fact that between 1956 and 1965 the share of raw materials and foodstuffs in the total exports of the Third World fell does not mean that these export sectors have decreased, but that their real growth has been overshadowed by the greater expansion in the sale of oil.

This should only give more weight to the growth of some 2 percent in exports of manufactured goods seen in the analysis of total exports (Table V-6B). But haven't we underestimated this progress because common metals have been incorrectly included in this category? It can be claimed that if, between 1956 and 1965, the proportion of manufactured goods in Third World exports increased, it increased even more in exports. Finally, how much of this increase in the Third World's sales of manufactured goods is due to Hong Kong's contribution (see above)? We must await clearer and more coherent figures before rejoicing.

4. Terms of Trade

Everyone is more or less aware that since the Second World War the prices of raw materials exported by the Third World have generally fallen or risen considerably less rapidly than those of the manufactured goods which that same Third World imports

---

[3] *Ibid.,* p. 131.

from the developed capitalist countries. This leads to a deterioration for the Third World, and an improvement for the developed capitalist countries, in what is known as the "terms of trade"—that is, in the relationship between the average unit value of exports and the average unit value of imports. In other words, the price the Third World receives for a given quantity of raw materials will serve to purchase less and less of this or that manufactured commodity. The International Center for Development published a report at the beginning of 1967 which pointed out: "In 1954, a jeep could be purchased with the value of fourteen bags of coffee; by 1962 it required thirty-nine."[4]

Of course, price movements are not parallel for all commodities in a particular category, and the changes in the average price for products in a given category are not uniform over time, any more than are changes in the terms of trade. For instance, in 1951–53 the Korean War led to sharp variations in the terms of trade between industrial countries and Third World countries, contrary to the general trend. There are also periods of relative stability, as in 1963–65.

We have chosen to examine the unit value of exports and the terms of trade for the years 1955 to 1965 (Tables V-8A and B), with the combined purpose of covering a recent period, one sufficiently long to be significant (ten years) but short enough to eliminate the irregularities that accompanied and immediately followed the Korean War.

It can be seen that during these ten years the unit value of the exports of the developed capitalist countries grew by 7 percent, while it fell by 8 percent for the Third World. What is gained by one group is lost by the other, so that over the same period, taking as a base 1958 = 100, the terms of trade are found to have improved from 96 to 104 (+ 8 percent) for the developed capitalist countries and deteriorated from 108 to 97 (−11 percent) for the Third World taken as a whole. By major regions, the adverse change was 15 percent for Africa, 13 percent for Latin America,

---

[4] *Le Monde,* March 8, 1967. The Center is a semi-official body guided by Josué de Castro, president and founder, and Maurice Guernier, secretary general.

8 percent for the Middle East, and 7 to 8 percent for South and
East Asia.

Many learned treatises and debates have been devoted to the
possible or probable causes of a situation so alarming for the
Third World. Almost all these overlook the fundamental cause
which ultimately lies in a power relationship unfavorable to the
Third World. We saw in the previous section that raw and semi-
raw materials constitute nine-tenths of the Third World's exports,
and that, for many Third World countries, one, two, or three products provide 50 to 98 percent of receipts from external trade. How
could such countries be in a position of strength in relation to
buyers or groups of buyers to whom these same products represent only a very small proportion of their imports? They could be
so only by setting up absolutely solid common fronts, which is
not yet the case. Doubtless international organizations have de-
bated the problem of organizing markets and stabilizing the prices
of basic products, and the United Nations Conference for Trade
and Economic Development met in Geneva in 1964 with the
official purpose of solving this problem. Like so many conferences
and like the few international agreements on basic products (wheat,
sugar, tin, olive oil, coffee) reached under the aegis of the United
Nations, this meeting produced only the disappointing results
which were carefully analyzed in *The Pillage of the Third World*.
It could not but produce disappointing results since only the very
naive could imagine that under present conditions international
organizations can provide a framework for truly free and equal
discussion between the rich and the poor nations. In the orbit of
imperialism, in the economic field as in all others, power relations
are always the final determinant of events.

In this respect, the data in Table V-9A are curious. They show
the changes between 1960 and 1966 in the export prices (base
1958 = 100) of basic products for the developed areas and for
the "developing" areas. The general index for primary commodities rose from 99 to 111 (+ 12) for the developed areas but
dropped from 94 to 93 for the underdeveloped areas. For foodstuffs, there was an increase from 98 to 112 (+ 4) for the developed countries and only from 84 to 89 (+ 5) for the under-

developed. For other agricultural products, $+ 9$ and $- 3$ are the respective changes; for minerals, $+ 9$ and $+ 2$. The only exception is in the category of non-ferrous base metals, for which the rise for the developed countries $(+ 41)$ falls short of that for the underdeveloped $(+ 91)$.

Within each category the products for each group of countries are doubtless not always the same. But the size and regularity of the discrepancies, with only one exception, illustrates the fact that the rich, strong countries defend the prices of their basic products far more effectively than do the weak, poor countries. Paul Bairoch[5] has recorded that between 1952–54 and 1961–65 the price of wheat moved much more favorably than that of rice; that the price of beet sugar increased or remained stable while the price of cane sugar fell (in spite of the international agreement on sugar); that butter prices rose and vegetable oil prices fell; and that the prices of fruit from temperate climates rose sharply while those of tropical fruits rose only very slightly.

Many observers have tried to evaluate the losses suffered by the Third World as a result of the deterioration of the terms of trade and many, with varying approaches, have analyzed these losses as a spoliation to be balanced against the economic "aid" received by the Third World. It will suffice to quote once more from the report of the Center for International Development:[6] "It has been calculated that the benefits thus gained by the rich countries which import these commodities were equal to or greater than the \$8 billion in aid which they gave to the Third World. Thus aid contributes nothing to development, but serves only to plug a hole as fast as it is being dug open." François Luchaire[7] regards aid as a form of "restitution," and even the very official report from M. Jeanneney[8] sings a similar tune.

Hence it is of great interest to try to evaluate the losses suffered

---

[5] Bairoch, *op cit.*

[6] *Le Monde,* March 8, 1967.

[7] François Luchaire, *L'Aide aux pays sous-développés,* Collection Que Sais-je? (Paris: Presses Universitaires de France, 1966), p. 19.

[8] Jeanneney is chairman of a committee of experts which prepared a report to the French government on its aid to underdeveloped countries and ways of improving it.—*Trans.*

through the depreciation of the Third World's exports and the ever-rising cost of its imports, since, whatever reasons various observers may suggest for the phenomenon, all agree that it is the industrialized capitalist partners who profit by it. Taking as a starting point the situation as it was about fifty years ago, François Luchaire estimates the losses suffered by the Third World on its 1965 exports at $14 billion. Using a more recent base (1954), Paul Bairoch calculates the reduction in the terms of trade in such a way as to eliminate the circumstantial elements during the first part of the period, and concludes that the terms of trade worsened by 12 percent between 1954 and 1965, leading to a loss of resources of the order of $4.3 billion in 1965.[9]

Returning to Table V-8B, whose starting point is 1955—not exactly pre-history—the deterioration in the terms of trade for the Third World by 1965 appears to have been $108 - 97 = 11$. Applying this to the $36.7 billion-worth of Third World exports in 1965 gives a loss of $4,040 million.

Such a general estimate, like that made by Paul Bairoch, seems very rough in that it is applied to the trade of the Third World as a whole and includes the 21 percent which takes place between Third World countries. United Nations data,[10] always using the base $1958 = 100$, shows changes in the terms of trade between the Third World countries and the developed capitalist countries, calling them respectively Economic Class I and Economic Class II. These terms of trade fell from 110 in 1955 to 93 in 1963. Since they were stable between 1963 and 1965 (but fell again in 1966) this 17 point deterioration also applies to the period 1955–65. Applying this 17-point drop to Third World exports going only to the advanced capitalist countries in 1965 ($26,360 million) gives a loss of $4,481 million suffered by the Third World in its trade with the advanced capitalist countries. A round figure of $4.5 billion will be used in later references to this matter. It must be emphasized that this figure is calculated using 1955 as a base year and that this was not, alas, the year in which unequal trade began for the Third World. Charles

---

[9] Bairoch, *op. cit.*, p. 162.
[10] *United Nations Statistical Yearbook, 1965,* Table 152.

Bettelheim estimates that in the middle of the ten-year period 1950–60 the losses of the so-called underdeveloped countries in their terms of trade stood at $6 billion.[11]

5. Maritime Shipping

Table V-10 shows, for 1965, the division of the world's merchant fleet, by groups of countries, expressed in gross tonnage. The Third World comes in for only 6 percent when Liberia and Panama are quite properly excluded as being flags of convenience for the advanced capitalist countries. Thus the Third World pays those countries which transport most of its goods a heavy tribute in the form of maritime freight charges. It is not without interest to try to evaluate the cost, however rough such an estimate must be.

For world trade as a whole, the difference between the value of exports FOB and CIF is 5 percent. It is obvious, however, that this figure has no relevance to the countries of the Third World which carry on three-quarters of their trade with advanced capitalist countries very distant from most of them, making them liable to long and expensive sea transport. By assembling sample data and especially by using Tables 27 and 28 of the International Monetary Fund's 1966 annual report, it has been possible to estimate the difference between the FOB value and the CIF value of the 1964 imports for six Third World countries chosen from widely differing geographical areas. The differences are: Brazil, 16 percent; Pakistan, 12 percent; Morocco, 4.4 percent; Venezuela, 4 percent; the Philippines, 11 percent; and Ghana, 7 percent. These percentages are consistent, though that for Brazil seems a little high. The arithmetical mean for all six is 9 percent, which caution suggests should be reduced to 8 percent. When this 8 percent is applied to the $37 billion-worth of imports the Third World took in in 1965, the difference in value is $2.96 billion or, in round figures, $3 billion.

Unfortunately, no sufficiently reliable data could be found upon which to base a similar calculation for exports. It seems certain, however, that the incidence of freight charges on an infinitely larger tonnage must lead to a discrepancy between FOB and CIF

---

[11] Bettelheim, *op. cit.*, p. 38.

much more important for the totals. For example, in 1964 Africa shipped out 148 million tons of goods and received 67 million tons; for South America the figures were 242 million against 40 million; and for Asia 440 million tons against 290 million.[12] It seems reasonable to estimate that the FOB/CIF difference on Third World exports averages at least 12 percent, and this, applied to $36.7 billions worth of exports, gives a value gap of $4.4 billion.

The sum of the differences between exports and imports thus rises to $7.4 billion. We have reduced this to $7 billion to allow for the small proportion of Third World trade which may be carried on across frontiers by rail or road and cut a further 10 percent to eliminate the insurance and other subsidiary costs, leaving some $6.3 billion for actual freight charges.

If we admit that it would be legitimate for the Third World to perform half the maritime transport of the goods it imports and exports, it should derive $3.15 billion from transport. But since its merchant fleet only represents 6 percent of world tonnage and its external commerce only 20 percent of world trade, it can only use its own fleet for 30 percent of its own trade, representing receipts of $6 \times 0.3 = \$1.8$ billion. It is thus obliged to pay a tribute to the advanced capitalist countries in the form of maritime transport charges which can very grossly be estimated at a minimum of $\$3.15 - \$1.8 = \$1.35$ billion, a figure which is far from negligible and almost always overlooked as an aspect of the relations of dependence between the Third World and the developed capitalist countries.[13]

6. Summary and Critical Analysis

In the first section of this chapter and in Table V-1 we saw the share of the total world exports falling to each of our three major groups of countries in 1948, 1956, and 1965. Table V-2B gives the same information in terms of percentages. The per-

---

[12] *United Nations Statistical Yearbook, 1965,* Table 18.

[13] An argument based on using the merchant fleet of the Third World to transport only, but entirely, its own exports would be more favorable to my thesis, but this would be unrealistic in view of the role of "return charges" in maritime transport.

centage share of the developed capitalist group and the socialist group continued to progress at the expense of the Third World countries. On the other hand, the rate of growth of exports, as shown in Table V-2C for 1948–56 and 1956–58, was the same for the developed capitalist countries, declined for the socialist countries, and increased very slightly for the Third World countries (but the first period covers eight years and the second nine). It remains true, however, that during the second period the exports of the developed capitalist countries grew in value 81 percent faster than those of the Third World. From this situation conclusions are often drawn which assume a decrease in the economic weight of the Third World and a relaxation of the bonds of dependence of the underdeveloped countries on the developed capitalist countries, conclusions which are not acceptable without far more precise proof. Two major correctives should, in my view, be applied to the figures in Tables V-2B and C:

1. Just as it would be unseemly for a strong man who was starving a weak man to announce—and to display surprise—that the weak one had lost weight, it appears to us wrong in every sense to calculate the value of the Third World's exports at rates imperialism has arranged to pay, and which are below their just price. By adding to the total Third World exports for 1965 the $4.5 billion which the Third World lost in 1965 owing to the deterioration in the terms of trade—using 1955 as base—it can be estimated that between 1956 and 1965 Third World exports rose not by 48 percent but by 65 percent, a rate of growth much closer to that of the developed capitalist countries.

The matter can also be argued directly on the volume and not the value of exports. Table 151 of the *United Nations Statistical Yearbook, 1965,* taking $1958 = 100$ as a base, shows that the volume of exports from the developed capitalist countries rose from 97 in 1956 to 168 in 1965, and that from the Third World from 97 to 150. The growth is thus on the order of 71 percent for the former and 53 percent for the latter—that is, some 34 percent more rapid for the developed capitalist countries than for the Third World. This is a large gap but nothing like that in value, where the growth rate was 81 percent more rapid for the developed capitalist countries. But again, what is the real significance of the difference between the growth rates of the volume of the exports of the two groups of countries?

2. It would be good at this point to recall that the essence of trade—and the justification of its economic utility—is the exchange of a commodity for which the original owner has no use for one which he lacks and needs, and vice versa, with money serving as a bridge. It might well be asked to what extent trade among the advanced capitalist countries themselves still shows this essential characteristic and is justifiable on this basis.

The first thing to note is the extraordinary growth of this internal trade within the group of developed capitalist countries: up 106 percent from 1956 to 1965. This is quite out of step with the growth of their gross domestic product, up 37 percent from 1956 to 1964. What categories of goods provided this spectacular rate of growth?

A study of trade within the EEC offers a partial but very significant answer since in 1965 the internal trade of the EEC countries alone amounted to 21.5 percent of all trade between the developed capitalist countries. In the seven years from 1958 to 1965 total intra-EEC trade was multiplied by exactly three.[14] Table V-11 shows the rates of multiplication for different categories of goods. It is interesting to note that the rate for foodstuffs is slightly below the average growth rate and that for energy and raw materials distinctly lower, while those for all the industrial products are higher. But very much higher growth rates affect trade in certain more limited groups of products and sharpen our interest in carrying out a more detailed investigation. For this it has been possible to start with the statistics of French external trade, which is very typical of the developed capitalist countries.

Our figures cover exports and imports to and from all foreign countries outside the franc zone. Since France still has very little commerce with the socialist countries, and since its dealings with the Third World are predominantly within the franc zone, at least 90 percent, perhaps more, of all French trade with foreign countries outside the franc zone is conducted with other developed capitalist countries.

---

[14] *Statistique mensuelle des communautés européennes, 1966*, No. 12.

For cars, refrigerators, electro-mechanical domestic appliances, watches and clocks, footwear, cotton and woolen piece goods, clothing—taken as a group—imports from outside the franc zone rose from 214 million francs in 1956 to 2,026 million in 1964 (x 9.5), and exports from 634 million francs to 3,290 million (x 5.2). Over the same period, all French imports multiplied by 1.7 and exports by 1.9. The seven products listed above were chosen as being at first glance—without spending weeks sifting through all the French statistics—characteristic of a special expansion among consumer goods. These items alone actually provided 7.3 percent (more than half of this was cars) of the total value of French exports in 1964, which is not a negligible figure. The nature of the goods in which trade has grown so explosively should give food for thought, especially since in almost every case the trend recorded for exports and imports resulted in improving the French balance of trade for each product between 1956 and 1964. The improvement continued after 1964 and is still apparent.

There is an increasing propensity to trade more and more goods manufactured at home for similar goods from other industrial countries. This practice, which is not always limited to consumer goods, is facilitated by the greater openness of the frontiers between industrial countries and especially between partners in organizations like the EEC and the EFTA. But what is the economic benefit of such trade?

For instance the automobiles imported into France differ only in detail from those manufactured there. Both serve the same general purpose at the same cost. There will be little difference in the way the market is supplied whether ten or one hundred makes are available. Certainly, the abundance of different makes and models increases competition, goads the initiative of the manufacturers, and whets the appetite of the consumers. When all is said and done, however, there seems to be little economic benefit in exchanging a considerable quantity of similar cars with other industrial countries. The general level of demand and production are effected little, if at all. The motivation behind such trade is no longer need, or economic shortage, but is fundamentally fashion and snobbery, stimulated by advertising and by the diversity of goods that is carried to such absurd lengths in a consumer society. Starting with a conception of human needs clearly different from that of our Americanized Western society, it is possible to ask ourselves if the effort devoted to creating the transportation and sales network required to facilitate this reciprocal trade—trade which cancels itself out in the strict economic sense of the term—is not largely wasted. To stand in a frontier railway station and see a trainload of Volkswagen 1500's passing one of Peugeot 404's going in the opposite direction is very thought provoking.

In any case, this trade cannot possibly be measured by the same yardstick as the rigorously complementary and fundamentally important trade between the developed capitalist countries and the countries of the Third World. The problem here is a form of statistical conservatism which empties figures of their significance and falsifies comparisons. And the further question arises: at what point does trade within the EEC, for example, become something other than international, as tariffs and quotas are eliminated and as the more difficult task of harmonizing fiscal, social, and other charges proceeds? It is no mean paradox that trade between the two Italys, north and south, has much more of the character of international trade than has that between northern Italy and the remaining five of the "European Six."

It is obviously impossible to estimate how much of the internal trade between the advanced capitalist countries has been, since 1956, due to the more or less artificial kind of trade just examined in some detail. We have pointed out that this expansion has been facilitated by the EFTA and the Common Market, and L. Duquesne de la Vinelle was able to estimate that in 1964 the latter "created commerce" on the order of $4 billion[15]—that is, 9 percent of total imports (inside and outside the EEC) of the member nations in that year. He also notes, however, that between 1953 and 1958, before the Common Market came into operation, trade between the Six had increased by 75 percent, as

---

[15] *Informations Statistiques, 1965,* No. 4, published by the statistical bureau of the European community.

against 48 percent between the Six and the Third World. The growth of trade between the Six cannot, therefore, be credited solely to the Treaty of Rome, and it is certain that general conditions in the developed capitalist countries made the rapid growth in their trade over the last ten to twelve years possible, including that part of this expansion which is based wholly or partially on artificial exchanges.

Although the second cannot be measured, the two sets of data described above are offered as correctives to the figures for the growth of trade since 1956 for both the group of developed capitalist countries and those of the Third World. They appear to justify the doubts voiced by many about expressing in dollars trade which does not have the same economic significance for one party as the other. Our analysis would, however, be incomplete if we did not now pay attention to the fundamental problem of primary products.

The proposition is currently being put forward, often by reputable authors, that the industrialized capitalist countries are not only buying relatively less and less from the Third World countries, but, more especially, that they are buying less and less of their needs of raw materials and primary products. Such statements appear to be derived (the source is hardly ever given) from certain United Nations documents—the most detailed and explicit on this subject is certainly the *World Economic Survey, 1963,* Part I, particularly Chapter 5, "Access to Markets for Primary Commodities in the Industrial Countries." Table 5B-3 of this survey lists 140 products considered to be primary under the CTIC (Classification of Types for International Commerce), and is so extensive it cannot even be partially reproduced here. The data includes the percentage of total imports of each primary product imported by the industrial countries which, in 1962, originated from the "developing countries." These countries are identical with our Third World, except for the exclusion of South Africa, and the industrial countries correspond to our developed capitalist countries, with the single addition of Turkey.

One important reservation must be made about this important document: It treats the following as primary products (and these are only examples):

—Crude oil and oil products
—Metals and their ores
—Vegetable oils, their seeds, etc.

In other words, a product can be "primary" twice over: in its original state (as an ore, for example) and in the first or even second stage of its conversion (as a metal or an alloy). The CTIC classification ignores what are called "demi-products" or "semi-raw products" or, better, "intermediate products." This was their choice, but we can see where it leads.

1. Crude oil and oil products. The table referred to shows us that in 1962 the developing countries supplied the industrial countries with 92.7 percent of their total imports of crude oil (see our Table V-12A), but only 46.4 percent of their total imports of oil products—and 53.2 percent of this came from other sources. But where did the crude oil for this 53.2 percent come from? By far the largest exporter of oil products among the industrial countries is the United States, followed by some Western European countries that produce hardly any crude oil of their own. Even the U.S.A., although a major producer, is a net importer of crude oil. Without going into further detail, it clearly follows that the 53.2 percent of oil products imported by the industrial countries from "other sources" than the developing countries is largely, if not entirely, derived from crude oil imported from the Third World.

2. Aluminum and bauxite. In 1962 the developing countries supplied the developed capitalist countries with 86.8 percent of their bauxite but with only 3.5 percent of their primary aluminum which was, therefore, drawn almost entirely from other sources. But these industrialized countries mined only 17 percent of the world's bauxite (the socialist countries mined 22.5 percent) and among the major exporters of aluminum—Canada, U.S.A., Norway, France—only the latter was in a position to export aluminum derived from its own bauxite. It follows that all, or almost all, of the 96.5 percent of the aluminum imported by the industrialized countries that did not come from the developing countries came from among themselves—but at least four-fifths of it had been derived from the bauxite of the Third World.

Such examples could be multiplied, leading to similar conclusions. But things become very serious when the table referred to brings together the data for 140 so-called primary products, including those for bauxite and aluminum, and finally claims to determine the share of the developing countries in the primary products imported by the industrialized countries. Even so, the final figure is 43.8 percent. But this figure is of no significance as an indication of the real dependence of the developing capitalist countries on the Third World. Without the Third World's crude oil, the developed capitalist countries would have been able to refine and sell far fewer oil products to each other. Without the Third World's bauxite, they would have been able to refine only a fraction of the aluminum they sell to each other, and so on. The figures on which our analysis was based mask even further the reality that trade is expressed in value and that intermediate products are obviously far more highly priced than the truly primary items. This is pillage by statistics.

Much more could be said about the famous Table 5B-3: For instance, the heading "cocoa" includes cocoa powder and cocoa butter, which makes the Third World appear to contribute only 85.3 percent of the imports of the industrialized countries when it is practically the sole producer. Similarly, products such as lard, cut flowers and foliage, hay and forage, cheese and firewood, are counted as primary products! It is a serious matter that writers have accepted the validity of figures based on such work, or of others based on the same statistical classifications and combinations, or that they have swallowed undigested figures which incorporate an artificial reduction in the relative value of the exports of the Third World, and then have gravely concluded that the "colonial pact has disappeared."[16] But it is far more alarming when a Marxist economist like Ernest Mandel peremptorily declares that "the underdeveloped countries can serve less and less as a safety valve for the capitalist system as a whole."[17]

Others explain the supposed decline in the importance of the

---

[16] E. Bonnefous, *Les milliards qui s'envolent* (Paris: Librairie Artheme Fayard, 1963).

[17] E. Mandel, "L'apogée du néo-capitalism et ses lendemains," *Les Tempes Modernes,* August/September 1964.

Third World in the field of raw materials by the competition of substitute products, and they have for years been predicting the disappearance of cotton in favor of artificial fibers and synthetics, or that of natural rubber in favor of the synthetic product. Such competition certainly exists, but it did not prevent a 25 percent increase in world cotton production between 1956 and 1964 (42 percent in Third World production); nor did it prevent world natural rubber production from growing by more than 23 percent over the same period (see Table V-12B). These "dying" products are having a long life. Jean Vène explains that "it is impossible to envisage the complete replacement of natural rubber by the synthetic product," that "large quantities are required for certain purposes for which the natural product is irreplaceable," and also that certain improvements in the system of cultivation "will, in the near future, guarantee an essential place for natural rubber."[18]

We are told, and we ourselves predict, that plastics are, or will be, a threat to some metals and therefore to the original ores. But for one thing, it is too early to estimate the extent of any such threat and, for another, the principal raw material of plastics, as of synthetic textiles and rubber, is oil. Once the countries of the Third World have become economically emancipated, there will be nothing to prevent them from developing petro-chemical industries, especially since they are the source of the raw material. And this will reduce the industrial sector of the developed countries to a more just proportion. As for nuclear energy, which certainly presents a long-term threat to oil as a source of energy, the way in which the oil magnates always rush to pursue each new exploration and development shows this threat to be a very distant one.

Finally, is it true to say that the Third World is no longer a safety valve for the capitalist system as a whole? And, in the first place, is it still an essential outlet for the manufactured products of the developed capitalist countries?

We saw in Table V-1 that in 1965 these countries sent 21 percent of their exports—which means 2.2 percent of their gross

---

[18] *Caoutchouc et textiles synthétiques,* Collection Que Sais-je? (Paris: Presses Universitaires de France, 1961), p. 118.

domestic product—to the Third World. Of the total exports from the developed capitalist countries to the Third World, 79 percent, valued at $20,090 million, consisted of manufactured products. This was 6 percent of total manufactured production and is by no means a negligible quantity. It is not surprising that a newspaper article appeared entitled "The OECD Fears a Decline of Purchases by the Underdeveloped Countries from the European Nations."[19] This would not, however, be decisive by itself, and it is my contention that the dependence of the industrialized countries on the Third World does not lie here, but lies in the field of raw materials. If we question the summation in Table 5B-3 of the *World Economic Survey, 1963* and the conclusions that certain people, including its authors, have drawn from it, the calculations themselves can be accepted, especially those concerning individual products. Table V-12A has been extracted from these figures, and it shows that in all cases (except rubber, where the natural and synthetic products are listed together) the Third World contributes far higher percentages to the total imports of the developed capitalist countries than its share of world production. This is explained by the fact that its production of raw materials is almost all exported while the industrial countries usually begin by converting their own.

Since it is impossible for us to carry out similar calculations for years other than 1962, Table V-12B recapitulates the figures showing the growth of world production and the Third World's share in it for most of the raw materials mentioned above. In looking at these figures it must be remembered that between 1950 and 1953 massive stockpiling took place (because of the Korean War), while after 1957 (the thaw) the stockpiles were partially, but increasingly, liquidated. Let it be said in passing that this in itself bears witness to the importance the industrialized capitalist countries attach to the supplies that reach them from the Third World.

Throughout the period, and notwithstanding the hazards mentioned, the production of the raw materials listed grew constantly and often rapidly, with the exception of tin concentrate and lead

---

[19] *Le Monde,* August 27, 1965.

ore which have been more or less stagnant since 1956. Within this expansion of world production, the percentages produced by the Third World countries between 1956 and 1965 increased sharply for crude oil and iron ore (the European Coal and Steel Community was the world's biggest buyer), and also increased for cotton, manganese, copper, and bauxite. Percentages remained stagnant for phosphates and tin concentrate and declined for lead and zinc. It is worth noting that, in general, increasing Third World shares in production corresponded to large or very large increases in world production (except for phosphates, where there was an enormous increase in Soviet production), and that the Third World's share fell where world production was stagnant or declined (lead, tin—with zinc the exception). To put it another way, the Third World seems to be in an especially strong position in regard to products for which world demand is strongest, and this coincides with the products which are greatest in volume and importance: crude oil, bauxite, and iron ore.

On September 16, 1966, Mr. George D. Woods, then president of the World Bank, made a speech to the Council of Governors in which he said: "In ten years the ore production of the developing countries has increased by 10 percent, while in the industrial regions it rose by only 2 percent. The world is becoming more and more dependent on the combustibles and the metals which the developing countries are able to produce cheaply and abundantly."

For his part, Paul Bairoch notes that "between 1960 and 1964 imports of iron ore to the EEC countries from the underdeveloped countries rose from fifteen million tons to twenty-six million." He continues: "Similar, if not identical, expansion took place for most of the other products of the extractive industries," and he adds: "This growth is, moreover, likely to continue."[20]

For the present period the following data should be noted:[21] At its present rate of growth, world production of crude oil should double in the next ten years and nearly three-fifths of the recent expansion has taken place in the Middle East and Africa. Africa,

---

[20] Bairoch, *op. cit.*, p. 75.
[21] See Beaujeu-Garnier, *op. cit.*, pp. 56, 66, 67, 70, and 82.

which supplies only 6 percent of the world's bauxite, holds one-third of the reserves. The supply of copper is problematical in spite of a slight improvement in Katangese production in 1965 and the opening of two new deposits in Zambia: the price has risen by 13 percent, supplies fell by 40 percent, and consumption has, in fact, continued to grow. The world market for tin is still under-supplied, and U.S. government reserves are diminishing. Consumption of lead and zinc has exceeded production for the fourth successive year. The position in the market for manganese may become difficult: in a period of record demand, the United States has absorbed 35 percent of world production and surplus stocks have diminished sharply since 1957. The outstanding fact of 1965 is that the consumption of natural rubber began to increase again after two years of stagnation.

The least that can be said is that, for the present and in the short run, the raw materials of the Third World, and especially the products of its sub-soil (with the exception of cotton, for which one must strike a more pessimistic note), face very favorable conditions for a continuance and an acceleration of the growth already recorded.

A report prepared at the request of the French government entitled *Réflexions pour 1985*[22] offers data for long-term prospects for France, making special efforts to determine mineral requirements in 1985 in comparison with present consumption in order to elucidate a five year plan. Obviously almost all crude oil will be imported. For iron ore, imports will have to be about equal to home production. The authors point out that "technical developments seem to point to the use of less scrap iron to produce the same amount of steel." Imports will have to meet all requirements for copper, manganese, lead and zinc ores, and 50 percent of bauxite needs; phosphate imports will have to be at least trebled between 1963 and 1985.

Imported minerals supplied two-fifths of France's needs in 1961, but by 1985 imports may have to supply four-fifths, which would mean a five-fold increase. The report makes the further important point that "the economy of Europe as a whole will find

---

[22] *La Documentation française,* Paris, 1964.

itself in a similar position," and it concludes: "It seems unlikely that there will be any physical difficulty in obtaining imported mineral resources—world reserves of all the ores appear to be fully sufficient (with some uncertainty, however, about uranium, lead, and zinc)."

The report makes no suggestion as to the likely sources for these imports—increased five-fold not only for France but for the whole of Europe—presumably leaving this to others. But is the answer not implicit in the developments already described? *Réflexions pour 1985* merely offers confirmation in actual figures. Of course these are only forecasts, and the figures must be regarded as only broad orders of magnitude. It is nonetheless reasonable to state that within the next twenty years the factories of the imperialist countries will become infinitely more dependent on the Third World than they are today for raw materials and especially for products of the sub-soil.

We said "the factories of the imperialist countries," thus including those of the U.S.A. The view is widely held, though poorly documented, that this, the foremost industrial power in the world, possesses raw materials beneath its soil and reserve stocks which will keep it safe from all external dependence in this area for a long time to come. However, Harry Magdoff, in a recent and valuable study, presents a more exact picture of the situation:

> Even though United States business has always had to rely on foreign sources for a number of important metals (e.g., bauxite, chrome, nickel, manganese, tungsten, tin), it has nevertheless been self-reliant and an exporter of a wide range of raw materials until quite recently. This generalization has been a mainstay of those who argued that U.S. capitalism had no need to be imperialistic. But even this argument, weak as it may have been in the past, can no longer be relied on. The developing pressure on natural resources, especially evident since the 1940's, stirred President Truman to establish a Materials Policy Commission to define the magnitude of the problem. The ensuing commission report, *Resources for Freedom* (Washington, D.C., 1952), graphically summarized the dramatic change in the following comparison for all raw materials other than food and gold: at the turn of the century, the United States produced on the whole some 15 percent more of these raw materials than was domes-

tically consumed; this surplus had by 1950 turned into a deficit, with U.S. industry consuming 10 percent more than domestic production; extending the trends to 1975 showed that by then the overall deficit of raw materials for industry will be about 20 percent.[23]

Though the United States is relatively less dependent on the minerals of the Third World than are Western Europe and Japan, it is dependent too, and will be more so in the future. Doubtless the weight in dollars of raw materials and minerals seems small as a proportion of world exports, and perhaps it will not increase, but dollars and statistics in their present form do not adequately measure the links of dependence reflected in international trade. The Third World does continue to be the safety valve of the capitalist system and will be so increasingly in the future. We will return to this in the final chapter.

[23] See Harry Magdoff, *The Age of Imperialism* (New York and London: Monthly Review Press, 1969), pp. 195–96.

Table V-1

World Exports in 1948, 1956, and 1965 by
Groups of Countries and by Origin and Destination
(FOB value in million $U.S. current)

		Total exports	Exports to:					
			Developed capitalist countries		Socialist countries		Third World	
			Total	%	Total	%	Total	%
United States & Canada	1965	35,170	24,560	72	520	1.5	8,980	26.5
Western Europe	1965	79,010	61,950	79	3,670	4.5	13,030	16.5
Australia, New Zealand, South Africa	1965	8,450	4,330	51	480	6	3,650	43
Japan		5,330	4,110	78	310	6	860	16
Total developed capitalist countries	1965	127,960	94,960	75	4,970	4	26,510	21
Total developed capitalist countries	1956	68,370	45,890	69	1,700	2.5	18,950	28.5
Total developed capitalist countries	1948	36,520	23,700	65	1,490	4.0	11,320	31
U.S.S.R. and European socialist countries	1965	19,630	4,040	21	13,210	68	2,070	11
Asian socialist countries	1965	2,000	550	28	600	30	840	42
Total socialist countries	1965	21,630	4,590	21.5	13,810	65	2,910	13.5
Total socialist countries	1956	10,140	2,000	20	7,155	71	940	9
Total socialist countries	1948	3,690	1,530	41.5	1,720	46.5	440	12
Latin America	1965	11,170	7,990	72	900	8	2,230	20
Africa	1965	7,910	6,420	82	570	7	820	11
Middle East	1965	6,460	4,790	76.5	145	2.5	1,320	21
South and East Asia	1965	9,310	5,650	61	740	8	2,900	31
Total Third World	1965	36,710	26,360	73	2,350	6	7,570	21
Total Third World	1956	24,870	18,250	74	810	3	5,780	23
Total Third World	1948	17,300	11,780	68	480	3	5,040	29
World	1965	186,300	125,920	68	21,130	12	37,000	20
World	1956	103,400	66,140	65	9,665	9.5	25,670	25.5
World	1948	57,500	37,010	64	3,690	7	16,800	29

Note: South Africa is included in the developed capitalist countries and Cuba in the Third World (Latin America). Also note that for 1956 and 1965, total exports and world totals do not always correspond to the sum of their components; certain exports, among which are United States special category exports, are not shown. But our percentages are calculated on the sum of the components.

Source: United Nations Statistical Yearbook, 1965, Tables 149 and 152; United Nations Monthly Bulletin of Statistics, June 1966, Special Table B.

Table V-2

A. Gross Domestic Product and Exports of the Third World in 1965 by Regions (in percentages)

	GDP of the Third World	Exports from Third World
Latin America	34	32
Africa	.22	23
Middle East	7	18.5
South and East Asia	37	26.5
Total	**100**	**100**

Source: Figures calculated by the author.

B. Third World Percentage of Exports by Groups of Countries

	1948	1956	1965
Developed capitalist countries	63.5	66	68.5
Socialist countries	6.5	10	11.5
Third World	30	24	20

Source: Calculated by the author from Table V-I.

C. Percentage Growth of Exports by Groups of Countries

	1948-1956	1956-1965
Developed capitalist countries	+ 87	+ 87
Socialist countries	+ 174	+ 113
Third World	+ 44	+ 48

Source: Figures calculated by the author.

Table V-3

Relative Value of External Trade in 1964 as a
Percentage of Gross National Product
(in millions of $U.S.)

	Imports		Exports	
	Total	% GNP	Total	% GNP
United States	18,622	2.9	25,897	4.1
Canada	6,044	15.9	7,099	17.7
United Kingdom	15,438	16.7	12,341	13.4
West Germany	14,613	14.1	16,213	15.7
France	10,067	11.5	8,990	10.3
Italy	7,231	14.6	5,956	12.0
Netherlands	7,055	42.0	5,808	34.6
Bolivia	97	18	86	16
Chile	608	11	623	11
Guatemala	202	15	158	12
Mexico	1,458	8	1,036	6
Peru	571	22	667	26
Venezuela	1,119	16	2,742	39
Ghana	340	8	292	6
Morocco	456	18	432	17
Southern Rhodesia	238	26	233	26
South Africa	2,150	21	1,456	14
Tunisia	224	23	127	12
Zambia	120	20	441	73
Burma	256	16	231	15
Ceylon	415	27	394	26
Malaysia	819	34	909	38
Philippines	868	18	743	16
Turkey	542	7	411	5
South Korea	404	17	119	5

Source: For the developed capitalist countries: Basic Statistics of the EEC, 1965; for the Third World countries: calculated from Tables 148, 181, and 185 of the United Nations Statistical Yearbook, 1965.

Table V-4

Balance of Trade of the Major Regions of the
Third World in 1956 and 1965
(in millions of $U.S.)

	1956			1965		
	Imports CIF	Exports FOB	Balance	Imports CIF	Exports FOB	Balance
Underdeveloped regions, excluding South Africa	26,200	24,000	−1,300	37,600	36,500	−1,100
Latin America, including Cuba	7,930	8,640	+ 710	9,600	11,100	+ 1,500
Africa, excluding South Africa	6,790	5,650	−1,140	7,860	7,680	− 180
Middle East	3,270	3,930	+ 660	4,760	6,460	+ 1,700
South and East Asia	8,330	6,920	−1,410	12,480	9,310	−3,170

Note: Certain minor differences appear between the figures in this table and those in Table V-1.

Source: United Nations Monthly Bulletin of Statistics, February 1967, Table 52; United Nations Statistical Yearbook, 1965, Table 148.

Table V-5

Trade Between the Third World and the Developed Capitalist Countries in 1956 and 1965, Oriented by Major Regions

A. Exports from the Developed Capitalist Countries to the Third World (in millions of $U.S. FOB)

		Latin America		Middle East		South and East Asia		Africa	
		Total	%	Total	%	Total	%	Total	%
U.S.A. and Canada	1956	3,960	58	525	8	1,555	23	750	11
	1965	4,000	47.5	755	9	2,825	33.5	815	10
Western Europe	1956	2,060	20	1,470	14	2,495	25	4,130	41
	1965	2,680	22	2,100	17	2,960	24	4,520	37
Japan	1956	165	11	100	7	870	57	390	25
	1965	410	11.5	280	8	2,190	61.5	670	19
Australia, New Zealand, South Africa	1956	18		34		220		225	

B. Exports from the Third World to the Developed Capitalist Countries (in millions of $U.S. FOB)

		U.S.A. and Canada		Western Europe		Japan		Australia, New Zealand, South Africa	
		Total	%	Total	%	Total	%	Total	%
Latin America	1956	4,020	57	2,660	38	300	4	25	1
	1965	3,800	47.5	3,640	45.5	510	6	40	1
Africa	1956	600	13	3,820	83	80	2	105	2
	1965	640	10	5,470	85	180	3	130	2
Middle East	1956	335	12.5	1,910	71.5	185	7	230	9
	1965	470	10	3,120	65	890	18.5	310	6.5
South and East Asia	1956	1,100	27	2,035	51	600	15	300	7
	1965	1,790	31.5	2,290	40.5	1,190	21	380	7

Sources: United Nations Statistical Yearbook, 1965, Table 149; United Nations Monthly Bulletin of Statistics, June 1966, Special Table B.

95

Table V-6

A. Composition of Exports and Imports as a Percentage of the Total for the Developed Capitalist Countries and for the Third World in 1965

	Developed capitalist countries			Third World		
	Imports from all areas	Exports		Imports from all areas	Exports	
		All destinations	Destined for Third World		All destinations	Destined for the developed capitalist countries
Manufactured goods*	56.8	70.8 (1956: 63.1)	78.8 (1956: 77.4)	66.9 (1956: 62.7)	17.5 (1956: 13.3)	16.2 (1956: 11.8)
Combustible minerals and lubricants	10.1	3.2	1.6 (1956: 3.1)	8.7 (1956: 11.9)	30.4 (1956: 25.3)	31.9 (1956: 21.5)
Raw materials	15.1	10.8	5.0 (1956: 4.1)	6.9 (1956: 7.4)	22.8 (1956: 28.5)	23.6 (1956: 30.9)
Food	17.0	14.0	12.9 (1956: 12.8)	15.9 (1956: 15.9)	28.7 (1956: 32.3)	27.9 (1956: 35.1)
Totals	99.0	98.8	98.3	98.4	99.4	99.6

*This includes primary raw materials, which are about 6 percent of the total exports of the Third World.

Source: United Nations Statistical Yearbook, 1966, Table 151.

B. Third World Exports Adjusted for Metals

	Exports to all destinations	Exports to the developed capitalist countries
Manufactured goods	11.5 (1956: 9.3)	10.2 (1956: 7.8)
Combustible minerals and lubricants	30.4 (1956: 25.3)	31.9 (1956: 21.5)
Raw materials	28.8 (1956: 32.5)	29.6 (1956: 34.9)
Food	28.7 (1956: 32.3)	27.9 (1956: 35.1)
	99.4	99.6

Source: Calculated by the author from Table V-6A.

96

Table V-7

A. The Contribution of Agriculture to Exports in 1964
(in hundred thousand $U.S.)

	Value of all exports	Agricultural exports	
		Value	%
Argentina	14,104	12,945	92
of which meat		3,265	23
and cereals:		5,004	35
Brazil	14,298	12,396	87
of which coffee:		7,597	53
Columbia	5,480	4,329	79
of which coffee:		3,942	72
Cambodia	962	887	92
of which rice:		572	60
Ceylon	3,939	3,805	96
of which tea:		2,396	60
Pakistan	4,252	?	?
of which jute and hemp:		2,143	50
Ghana	2,921	2,529	86
of which cocoa:		1,907	65
Réunion	374	339	90
of which sugar:		316	84
Senegal	1,225	1,173	96
of which groundnuts and			
groundnut oil:		857	70
U.A.R.	5,354	3,965	74
of which raw cotton:		2,681	50
Syria	1,761	1,573	89
of which raw cotton:		807	50

Source: Food and Agricultural Organization Trade Yearbook, 1965, various tables.

B. The Contribution of Certain Products to the Exports
of Some Third World Countries
(in percentages)

Burma: rice + teakwood + metals and ores	= 79%
Bolivia: tin ore + lead ore + tungsten ore	= 74%
Chile: copper + nitrates + wood	= 76%
Indonesia: rubber + petroleum + oilseeds and oils	= 78%
Malaya: rubber + tin	= 64%
ex-Rhodesia/Nyasaland: copper + tobacco + asbestos	= 82%
Thailand: rice + rubber + tin ore	= 68%
Venezuela: petroleum + iron ore + coffee	= 98%
(averages 1959-1961)	

Source: World Economic Survey, 1963, Part I, Table 6-9.

Table V-8

A. Unit Value (Price) Index of Exports
(1958 = 100)

	1955	1960	1963	1965
Developed areas (developed capitalist countries and South Africa)	97	100	102	104
Underdeveloped regions (Third World except South Africa)	105	98	95	97
of which Africa:	103	94	92	94
Latin America:	111	95	94	101
Middle East:	94	91	89	89
Middle East, excepting petroleum:	99	95	95	95
Asia (sterling areas):	111	114	102	108
Asia (non-sterling areas):	106	105	101	103

B. Terms of Trade
(1958 = 100)

	1955	1960	1963	1965
Developed areas	96	103	104	104
Underdeveloped areas	108	99	97	97
of which Africa:	106	97	92	91
Latin America:	115	96	97	102
Middle East:	96	94	89	88
Middle East, excepting petroleum:	102	98	96	95
Asia (sterling areas):	112	110	103	104
Asia (non-sterling areas):	105	107	99	98

Sources: United Nations Statistical Yearbook, 1965, Table 16; United Nations Monthly Bulletin of Statistics, January 1967, Special Table A.

Table V-9

A. Indices of Export Prices
(1958 = 100)

		1960	1961	1962	1963	1964	1965	1966 three quarters
Primary commodities	A	99	100	99	105	109	108	111
	B	94	90	89	97	98	93	93
Food	A	98	98	100	107	111	111	112
	B	84	82	82	100	101	88	89
Agricultural non-food	A	102	103	99	104	108	106	111
	B	114	104	99	100	101	102	101
Minerals	A	96	97	97	99	102	105	105
	B	91	90	90	90	92	93	93
Non-ferrous base metals	A	111	108	106	106	128	143	152
	B	120	114	115	116	147	176	211

Note: A=Indices of exports of developed areas. B=Indices of exports of "developing areas."

Source: United Nations Monthly Bulletin of Statistics, December 1966, Special Table C-III.

B. Indices of Prices of Manufactured Goods
(1958 = 100)

	1960	1961	1962	1963	1964	1965	1966 three quarters
World exports of manufactured goods	101	102	102	103	104	106	109

Source: United Nations Monthly Bulletin of Statistics, December 1966, Special Table C-1.

Table V-10

Merchant Fleets in 1965
(in thousand gross registered tons)

United Kingdom	21,530
United States	21,527
Liberia*	17,539
Norway	15,641
Japan	11,971
Greece	7,137
Italy	5,701
West Germany	5,279
France	5,198
Total developed capitalist countries	c. 136,500
% world	85%
Soviet Union	8,238
Total socialist countries	c. 13,900
% world	9%
India	1,523
Argentina	1,289
Brazil	1,253
Total Third World	c. 10,000
% world	6%
World	**160,392**

*Liberia and Panama, "flags of convenience," are included in the developed capitalist countries. Liberia has recently become the world leader.

Source: United Nations Statistical Yearbook, 1965, Table 155.

Table V-II

Increase of Trade Within the EEC

Food	X 2.9
Energy	X 1.3
Raw materials	X 2.5
Machines and transportation equipment	X 3.55
of which transportation equipment	X 3.9
Other industrial products	X 3.2
of which thread, fabrics and textile articles	X 3.4
of which furniture, clothes and shoes	X 5.7

Source: Statistique mensuelle des communautés européenes, 1966, No. 12.

Table V-12

A. Contribution of the Third World to the Total Imports of the Developed Capitalist Countries for Certain Raw Materials in 1962

Cotton	61.2%	Iron	49.1%
Rubber (natural and synthetic)	75.5%	Manganese	74.1%
Wood (rough)	49.3%	Copper	57.8%
Jute	97.5%	Tin	85.5%
Crude Oil	92.7%	Zinc	45.9%
		Lead	42.7%
Phosphates	64.5%	Bauxite	86.8%

Source: World Economic Survey, 1963, Part 1, Table 5B-3.

B. Development of the Production of Certain Raw Materials and the Third World Share — 1948-1964 (in thousand metric tons except as marked)

		1948*	1956	1960	1962	1964
Raw cotton	WORLD	7,600	9,500	10,700	10,900	11,900
	% Third World	33%	37%			42%
Natural rubber	WORLD	1,550	1,920	2,020	2,165	2,275
	% Third World		100%			100%
Crude oil (million metric tons)	WORLD	467.1	839.6	1,054.2	1,216.6	1,410.1
	% Third World	34%	42%			51.6%
Natural phosphates	WORLD	17,100	28,600	33,500	36,900	44,100
	% Third World		40%			39%
Iron ore (million metric tons)	WORLD	103.5	186.7	230.9	242.5	281.2
	% Third World		15%			25%
Manganese ore	WORLD	2,200	5,000	5,500	6,000	6,600
	% Third World		44%			47%
Copper ore	WORLD	2,250	3,140	3,840	4,030	4,220
	% Third World		47.5%			52%
Tin Concentrates	WORLD	148.7	169.1	138.7	143.9	149.5
	% Third World		96%			95%
Zinc ore	WORLD	1,800	2,800	2,960	3,130	3,400
	% Third World		27%			24%
Lead ore	WORLD	1,360	1,910	1,940	2,050	1,990
	% Third World		35%			32%
Bauxite	WORLD	8,430	17,870	25,100	27,640	29,510
	% Third World		64%			68%

*The figures given for cotton and rubber refer not to 1948 but to the yearly averages
*The figures given for cotton and rubber refer not to 1948 but to the yearly averages 1948-1952.

Note: The world totals are taken unaltered from the reference tables. In some cases, they exclude a certain number of countries, particularly from the socialist world.

Source: United Nations Statistical Yearbook, 1965, various tables.

Chapter VI

Movements of Capital and Aid to the Third World

This chapter will be divided into three sections:

1. Aid to the Third World
2. United States Private Investment
3. The Return Flow of Capital

The most complete list—as we shall see, even too complete—ment of capital going to the Third World from the rich nations; the third section deals with capital movement in the reverse direction, which is often overlooked but nevertheless merits special attention.

1. Aid to the Third World

The most complete list—as we shall see, even too complete—of the various types of aid or economic assistance to the Third World appears in documents put out by the DAC (Development Assistance Committee), a body set up in 1960 under the aegis of the OECD. Table VI-1 reproduces the essential data for 1960, 1963, 1964, and 1965. Note 2 to this table shows that the DAC is comprised of almost all the developed capitalist countries involved in aid to the underdeveloped countries.

Only a small portion of aid comes from countries which are not members of the DAC (see the last line of the table) and this consists mainly of aid from the socialist countries, which the 1965–66 annual report of the World Bank estimates at $500 million for each of the years 1964 and 1965. This socialist aid is obviously public, and is mainly composed of loans bearing an interest rate of 2.5 percent. Almost half of it is designated for the industrialization of the receiving countries.

But since our main object in this book is to study the economic relations between the Third World and the developed capitalist countries, our attention will be centered on aid coming from the latter.

The figures in Table VI-1 show that between 1960 and 1965, according to the DAC, the total aid given by its member countries rose from $7,950 million to $10,150 million, an increase of 27.7 percent at current prices. Over the same period the gross national product of the OECD countries as a whole grew by 27 percent but at constant prices.[1] This period was the first half of the famous "development decade" during which a special effort was to be devoted to economic aid to the Third World, and it can be seen that, at constant prices, this aid grew distinctly more slowly than the gross national product of the givers (price increases of 2.5 percent per annum). Thus it declined in relative value. The net total of financial resources supplied by the industrial countries of the OECD to the less developed countries and multilateral organizations changed as follows (in percentage of their national income): 1960, 1.19 percent; 1961, 1.23 percent; 1962, 1.06 percent; 1963, 1 percent; and 1964, 0.97 percent—a drop from 1.19 to 0.97 percent.

But more exact figures can be found for the total aid given by the member countries of the DAC by scanning its component elements, which are all given in net values—that is to say, with amortization charges deducted. The first line gives reason to pause: technical assistance was valued at about $1 billion in 1964. If one is speaking in terms of the flow of capital it must be remembered that certain countries giving aid usually pay the salaries of technical advisers and assistants into accounts open to them in their home countries, from which they draw and transfer only what they require to live on in the country in which they are working. The remainder, often a considerable sum, becomes savings. In other

---

[1] *Croissance économique 1960–1970,* OECD, 1966, p. 22.

cases, salaries are paid partly in the assisted country and partly in the country of origin. It must also be noted that, because of special pay for overseas service and other allowances, technical assistants are overpaid. Without for the moment considering the question of the often doubtful effectiveness of the aid, it must be admitted that the figures are inflated, though it is impossible to estimate the extent.

The problem is far simpler when it comes to the reparations and indemnities paid by Germany, Italy, and Japan. It is almost indecent to put these "reparations" under the heading of aid and they must be eliminated altogether. Loans "reimbursable in local currency" call for only one comment: that after all they are loans and not gifts and should be listed with the former and not the latter. The case of sales payable in local currency is more complicated: these consist solely of the sale by the U.S.A. of surplus agricultural products to be paid in the currency of the buyer, which is often not convertible. Part of the receipts, however, go toward United States diplomatic or military expenses in the importing country, which means that if such sales do not bring in convertible currency they do enable the United States to avoid dollar transfers to pay for their embassies or bases. The proportion of receipts devoted to U.S. government costs varies and a serious estimate is also difficult here.

We now jump to private loans and investments in order to dispute the inclusion of "reinvested profits" under aid. This is the portion of profits made by foreign enterprises in the Third World which is reused on the spot, usually for auto-financing. In 1964–65, these reinvested profits only came to 14 to 15 percent of total profits made by private investment in the Third World—and 20 percent of revenues made from direct investment; they cannot be regarded as internal savings since they do not bring any fresh currency to the country in which the investment is made. It might be argued that they prevent the export of currency for the transfer of said profits which would have occurred if there had been no reinvestment. This overlooks the fact that most of this reinvestment is due to legislation in the host country permitting only part of the profits to be transferred. If this reinvestment had been chosen by the foreign enterprise and served its interest, it would have been obliged to import currency if the profits had not been on hand. Purely and simply, this heading should be removed from the list of aid to underdeveloped countries.

Now comes the category of private export credits, and these are almost always guaranteed by the states from which the exporting firms originate. Since France is the developed capitalist country which uses such credits most extensively, an examination of its system will serve well as an example. First, we should note that French legislation on export credits antedates the appearance of the Third World and the concept of aid to it: the Compagnie Française d'Assurance pour le Commerce Extérieur (COFACE), which specializes in these operations, was set up by a decree of June 1, 1946, applying a law of September 2, 1945. Pamphlets on export credit guarantees issued by COFACE in 1960 and 1967 make absolutely no distinction between the different countries which receive the exports benefiting from the credits, and these are in no way reserved for underdeveloped countries. The same is true of a document published in 1965 by the Centre National du Commerce Extérieur (CNCE), except that here credits for periods exceeding five years are reserved "for major operations concerning heavy equipment for industrializing countries." Finally, in February 1967 a government-sponsored congress was held on foreign trade, dealing mainly with the financing of exports. This was fully reported in *Le Monde* on February 10 and 11. Nowhere in this account is there even a passing reference to any aid to the Third World, but it does contain the idea of "aid to the export trade" and is full of references to international competition. This is really the heart of the matter and all credits, encouragement, and aid to exports form part of an arsenal of measures designed to strengthen the hand of export firms in facing competition in all the world's markets, including those of the United States and the socialist countries. Must we conclude that France is giving aid to the U.S.A., to the U.S.S.R., and to China?

All the industrialized capitalist countries practice similar policies, using the same kind of measures, and this creates a sort of auction in national aid to exports. The 1965–66 World Bank

report even condemns the inflation of such credits while it nevertheless considers that the rates of interest are often too high.[2]
However this may be, it is difficult to regard export credits as a
proper part of aid to the Third World. It has been shown that they
were not created or developed for this purpose, and if the underdeveloped countries benefit from them as much, or perhaps
even more, than other countries, this is because their markets are
an especially attractive field for exporters, particularly if they deal
in heavy equipment. Although the OECD report is presenting a
brief for existing aid, it states that these credits carry "conditions
which are among the most onerous,"[3] that they give rise to "a sort
of unfair competition" on the part of lender-exporters, and goes
so far as to add, "in so far as export credits are used to finance
development . . . ," a qualification which, in such a document,
bears the mark of a confession. *Le Monde* of August 13 and 14,
1967, analyzed a report from a commission of the EEC that con-
stituted a world index (excepting the United States) of such terms
under the heading "Credits for more than five years play an
essential role in the policy of the exporting nations" and the sub-
heading "Unfortunately they benefit the rich customers more than
the underdeveloped nations."

The balance can now be drawn. According to the DAC, aid
granted by its members in 1965 totaled $10,150 million, from
which the following should be deducted:

Reparations and indemnities	$ 141 million
Reinvested private profit	$ 836 million
Export credits	$ 741 million
Total	$1,718 million

Looking back to Table VI-1, it can be seen that the DAC
includes several southern European countries and Israel among
the recipients of aid for less developed countries. In 1964 these

---

[2] Gohran Olin, in *Aide et Endettement* (OECD, 1966, p. 36), suggests
that these rates "sometimes reach very high levels, on the order of 10 to
15 percent.

[3] *Development Assistance Efforts and Policies, op. cit.*

latter received bi- and multilateral public aid from DAC countries amounting to $462 million,[4] which makes a figure of $500 million a reasonable estimate for 1965, to which private investments in these countries must be added, particularly important in Spain. Thus a further sum of at least $600 million should be deducted.

On the other hand, it is fair to add both what accrued as the share of the non-socialist, non-DAC countries in the last classification of Table VI-1—that is, some $175 million—and also the $131 million additional multilateral contributions, making a total of $306 million. So the total aid to the Third World from all the developed capitalist countries in 1965 amounted to: $10,150 million — ($1,718 million + $600 million) + $306 million = $8,138 million, which we could reduce to $8 billion to allow for the increase, certain but not appraisable, due to the inclusion of "technical assistance" and "sales payable in local currency."

It is remarkable that this figure of $8 billion is the very one reached by the International Center for Development in a manifesto,[5] although we do not know whether or not the same calculations were used. In any event, this $8 billion represents about 0.78 percent of the national income or 0.70 percent of the gross domestic product of the countries giving aid, and 3.5 percent of the gross domestic product of the recipients. Guy-Willy Schmeltz maintains that "to raise the national income of the proletarian nations by 2 percent per annum would require annual investments at a rate equal to 25 percent of the actual gross product over the next twenty-five years,"[6] allowing for the population growth rate. If this view is accepted it becomes apparent that the rich capitalist countries are only giving the poor ones 14 percent of what would be necessary to reach a very modest target, and that is always supposing that the aid were to be used with perfect efficiency and to be quite without strings, both of which are far from being the case.

The aid given by the developed capitalist countries to the

---

[4] *Geographical Distribution of Financial Flows to Less-Developed Countries,* OECD, 1966.

[5] *Le Monde,* March 8–9, 1967.

[6] Guy-Willy Schmeltz, *L'Économie du tiers monde* (Paris: La Colombe, 1965), p. 57.

Third World is composed approximately as set out in Table VI-2A. In 1964–65 the bulk of the aid was drawn from the advanced capitalist countries in the proportions shown in Table VI-2B.

France and the United States (this last the only country giving repayable loans and making sales payable in local currency) gave relatively more gifts and less public loans than the others. They also made more direct private investment than the others (U.S.A., about 60 percent of all new investments; France, 15 to 20 percent). The United States supplied from 55 to 62 percent of the total resources of international aid institutions, followed by the United Kingdom (about 10 percent) and France (5 percent).

The distribution of aid, with the exception of private investment, by regions in 1960 and 1964 is shown in Table VI-3. The figures have been taken unadjusted from an OECD document. Since the totals do not correspond exactly to those shown in Table VI-1, which were also taken from OECD sources, they must be regarded as approximations. But this does not make the lessons to be drawn from them any less interesting.

From public bi- and multilateral funds in 1964, Latin America received $4.30 per head of population, Africa $5.90, and Asia $2.90. Looking at the changes between 1960 and 1964, Latin America gained considerably while the African and Asian shares both fell in relative value.

However, within the three continents sharp disparities can be observed between countries receiving aid. In 1964, South Korea received $170 million and South Vietnam $244 million ($414 million in all) of the $725 million allocated as bilateral aid to thirteen Far Eastern nations. For South Vietnam this was not all: in the fiscal year 1965–66 it received $590 million in economic aid from the United States alone, gaining the lead over India, which received only $310 million.[7] Aid to South Vietnam alone amounted to more than one-fifth of all the economic aid given by the United States.[8] A *Le Monde* dispatch from New Delhi reported that: "The new principles governing aid given by the United States in the form of food supplies have been the subject of severe criti-

---

[7] *Le Monde,* August 30, 1966.

[8] For 1967–68, South Vietnam will receive more United States economic aid than the whole of Africa.

cism here. Some commentators even see in them a form of pressure by which Washington wants to 'punish' India for refusing to support the American cause in Vietnam."[9]

These facts and figures show how much public aid to the Third World is politicized. A great deal of attention was devoted to this point—it is no longer much in dispute—in my earlier book, together with an extended critique of the effectiveness of aid. No more need be said here save to quote J. Suret-Canale on the subject of French bilateral public aid: "Between 1959 and 1962, 0.15 percent of the aid given by the FAC [Fund for Aid and Cooperation] went to the West African states for industrialization in the true sense."[10] It is worth recalling that about half the aid from the socialist countries is devoted to industrialization.

Suret-Canale also criticizes *The Pillage of the Third World* for the absolute distinction made between public aid and investment of private capital going from the capitalist countries to the underdeveloped countries. He makes the observation that under capitalism the motives for the two forms of aid are the same, and here I agree. On this subject Harry Magdoff quotes Eugene R. Black, the former president and chairman of the World Bank and an expert on the subject, as follows: ". . . our foreign aid programs constitute a distinct benefit to American business. The three major benefits are: (1) Foreign aid provides a substantial and immediate market for United States goods and services. (2) Foreign aid stimulates the development of new overseas markets for United States companies. (3) Foreign aid orients national economies toward a free enterprise system in which U.S. firms can prosper."[11]

It is, nevertheless, still correct to say that on the one hand private investments make possible a more searching analysis of the motives of imperialist action in the Third World and that, on the other hand, they have particular and extensive effects upon the movement of capital. Up to now they have been discussed as part of overall aid, but we will give them special attention, in particular United States investments.

---

[9] *Le Monde,* January 6, 1967.

[10] "Les rapports de la France et du tiers monde," *Démocratie Nouvelle,* December 1966.

[11] Magdoff, *op. cit.,* p. 176.

2. American Private Investment

We have seen that in 1964 and 1965 new American direct private investment in the Third World was some 60 percent (against 50 percent in 1963) of the total investment of that nature by the developed capitalist countries. Moreover, private United States bilateral investment in the Third World reached 45 percent of the total in 1963, 61 percent in 1964, and 68 percent in 1965. This new private American investment is thus very representative of the whole, since it is greater in volume than all others, is still growing, and anyway, as everyone knows, today it is the United States that sets the pace.

Table VI-4 gives the accumulated total of direct private American investment in various regions at the end of 1960, 1962, 1963, and 1964. It also shows the distribution of American investments by regions and by economic sectors at the end of 1964. It in effect presents, for the same years and the same groupings, the corresponding annual repatriated income.

It is thus possible to conclude that in 1964 33 percent of worldwide United States private direct investments was in the Third World—this is, $15 billion out of a total investment of $44.35 billion. Between 1960 and 1964 worldwide United States private capital investments grew by almost 36 percent, but those in the Third World grew by barely 20 percent. This confirms the already widely known fact that in recent years private United States capital, like that of the other developed capitalist countries, has been concentrated in these latter countries rather than in the Third World. The main explanation of this phenomenon can be found in the analysis of United States investments by regions and sectors of economic activity. Of all American capital invested in the developed capitalist countries, 49.5 percent has gone into manufacturing industries, and to this must be added most of the 24.6 percent which went into oil, since—except in Canada—this is for refining rather than extraction. This makes a total of 63–64 percent invested in industry. In the Third World, on the contrary, less than 22 percent of total investment was in manufacturing, while more than 55 percent was in mining and oil, in this case almost all extraction. Another point to remember is that three-quarters of United States manufacturing investments in the Third World are in Latin America. Harry Magdoff states that: "This investment is mainly in light manufacturing industry, including the processing of native food materials. Manufacturing operations in the durable goods field, such as autos, takes the form of assembly plants. This guarantees the export market of components and parts. It also contributes to stabilizing the market for these United States products."[12]

It is thus apparent that imperialist private capital has a far greater tendency to make investments in the developed capitalist countries in order to industrialize them further, rather than to make them in the Third World for its industrialization. When investment does, nevertheless, take place in the Third World, it is only to consolidate or conquer markets. Referring to United States private investments in Latin America, Guy-Willy Schmeltz writes: "The sectors in which private initiative occurs are chosen for immediate returns and are rarely essential, when they are not damaging, to the economic progress of the underdeveloped nation."[13] The factories so established "constitute isolated, watertight islands in the surrounding sea of underdevelopment."[14] He also refers to the general problem of the industrialization of the Third World with the aid of foreign capital and asks: "In any case, why should a business act so as eventually to deprive itself of its resources in raw materials and its outlets for finished goods by setting up, in a proletarian state, the very conversion industry which would consume and produce the latter?"[15]

What is of greatest concern to imperialist capital in the Third World is crude oil, raw materials, and, above all, minerals. But oil fields and mineral deposits cannot be found to order and, even when they are known to exist, why exploit them beyond immediate needs? This accounts for the slower growth of private investment in the Third World than in the independent capitalist world. There are, doubtless, other factors which contribute to the growth of the investments of the developed capitalist countries in

---

[12] *Ibid.*, pp. 199–200.
[13] Schmeltz, *op. cit.*
[14] *Ibid.*, p. 99.
[15] *Ibid.*, p. 59.

one another: the race for monopolistic concentration, the desire of United States capitalism to set itself up as a super-imperialism dominating the industrial countries themselves and, through them, the whole world. To return to the Third World, there is again little doubt that political conditions in many are such as to make prospective foreign investors nervous and cause them to hesitate or withdraw in spite of the attraction of possible profits. And these are indeed tempting.

We can calculate from Table VI-4 that in 1964 the repatriated profits on direct American investment amounted to about 5 percent on capital invested in the developed capitalist countries, and almost 16 percent on that invested in the Third World. It is possible that reinvested profit, which obviously does not appear as repatriated revenue, was higher in the former countries than the latter. Royalties and repayments derived from direct investment, which amounted to $909 million in 1965 and which do not appear in Table VI-4, were doubtless higher from the developed capitalist countries than from the Third World. The fact remains, however, that U.S. investments abroad bring in a far higher return in the Third World than elsewhere. Adding the $2,363 million revenue from direct investment repatriated from the Third World in 1964, and the $281 million reinvested in the same year,[16] the return on U.S. capital invested in the Third World amounts to 17.6 percent —and this is without allowing for an unknown amount for royalties and repayments. The total is probably not much below 20 percent.

Table VI-4 also shows that direct private American investments in the Third World grew by $900 million in 1964 (including reinvested profits), while repatriated revenue grew to $2,363 million— that is, by 2.6 times. If reinvested profits are excluded and only new investments bringing in dollars are considered, repatriated revenue appears to be 3.9 times greater.

It might be thought that although this loss of currency through private investment is catastrophic for the Third World (see the following section) it would be of little importance to the economies of the countries which export private capital. However, Harry Magdoff calculates that while revenue from United States

---

[16] *Development Assistance Efforts and Policies,* Table VI.

investment in all foreign countries in 1950 supplied about 10 percent of the profits of American companies (excluding finance companies) after taxes, by 1964 foreign sources of profit supplied 22 percent. In that year the Third World provided 64 percent of the profits from direct United States investments abroad, so that it may be estimated that the revenue which private capital derived from Third World countries came to some 14 percent of the profits made by United States companies (excluding finance companies) after taxes. Harry Magdoff explains that the data available to him tend to undervalue profits derived from abroad.[17]

Various other observations could be deduced from Table VI-4, particularly with regard to United States private investments by regions of the Third World and by sectors of their economies selected for investment. So that this section should not become too drawn out, we leave the curious reader to pursue these investigations. However, one last comment is called for: from 1960 to 1964 inclusive, private United States investment grew by 11.3 percent in Latin America, by 76 percent in Africa, and by 34 percent in Asia. Of the $2,522 million newly invested over these four years in all these regions, $1,047 million was in Latin America, $704 million in Africa, and $771 million in Asia. These figures seem to suggest that United States imperialism was seeking the geographical diversification of its private investments in the Third World. Since we saw in Section 2 of the preceding chapter a similar effort to diversify United States exports, these two harmonious trends are a concrete indication of the will of Yankee imperialism to increasingly impose its yoke on the entire Third World at the risk of slowing down the export of capital and commodities to Latin America, which is already powerfully dominated by the United States.

3. The Return Flow of Capital

With regard to United States private capital, the above has shown the importance of the return flow in the form of dividends transferred from the Third World to the United States. For the

---

[17] Magdoff, *op. cit.*

investing capitalist nations as a whole the 1965–66 World Bank report estimates this return flow of investment revenue at "more than $4 billion" coming from the developing countries. Table VI-5 is an attempted analysis on the basis of IMF (International Monetary Fund) documents. We arrive at a total for recorded transfers, for the revenue from various forms of private capital, amounting to $4,312 million in 1964. However, the data are missing for various African and Asian countries including some, like Indonesia and Congo-Kinshasa, which would make a considerable contribution to this total. We therefore estimated that a total for the Third World would be about $4,900 million.

We then proceeded to test this in reverse by setting out the position with regard to investment revenue for each of the developed capitalist countries, extracting the data from the same document, on the same basis, and for the same year. Thus the revenue which accrues from investments made with one another cancels out, and the overall balance of these countries shows their position with regard to the Third World. The result, shown in Table VI-6A, gives a net balance of $4,905 million for the developed capitalist countries. In the same year (see Table VI-1), new direct private investments and portfolio investments by the developed capitalist countries in the Third World represented a gain in private foreign currency of $1,575 million. But these very investments have meant the flight of profits of $4.9 billion—that is, 3.1 times more. This is why our severe view of aid in general as practiced by imperialism becomes downright condemnation when it comes to private investment.

Table VI-1 shows net figures for all movement of capital constituting aid to the Third World—after allowing for amortization and capital repayments. But interest payments on loans are not included. Table VI-6A shows the importance of the bilateral loans of the DAC countries. It is necessary to add to these figures the small amount of interest on loans paid to the rich countries which are not members of the DAC and the larger sum of interest on multilateral loans. Most of these are arranged by the World Bank and bear an interest rate at a minimum of 5.5 percent and a maximum of 6.25 percent. It appears that the total interest on bi-

The Third World in World Economy

and multilateral loans in 1964 can be assessed at a round figure of $500 million.

Export credits were excluded from aid properly so-called, but they cannot, unfortunately, be left out when the return flow of capital is under consideration since they are an important item in this category. The 1965–66 World Bank annual report states that "while statistics on the subject are far from complete, it appears that export credit may account very roughly for a quarter of the developing countries' total outstanding debt. The share of such credit in annual debt service is of course much higher because of the prevalence of relatively short maturities; it may approach half the total" (p. 34).

As for other loans, Table VI-1 shows net figures for export credits with amortization deducted. But the charge pertaining to the interest on these credits does not appear. It is possible, however, to try the following approach: in 1964 the total unamortized debt of the Third World countries was on the order of $29 billion. According to the World Bank, the share of this debt due to export credit guarantees was one-quarter, giving a figure of $7.2 billion. Taking the average interest rate to be 8 percent, which is conservative in the light of data given on this subject, annual interest charges can be estimated at $576 million, and this can safely be raised to $600 million to allow for credits not guaranteed.

It is now possible to set up Table VI-6C, which shows the drain from the Third World countries to the developed capitalist countries in 1964 through private dividends and profits, as well as interest on loans on credits. The final figure of $6 billion is surely an underestimate, not only because of the caution exercised in making the calculations, but also because only official transfers have so far been considered. As we showed in *The Pillage of the Third World,* when the subsidiaries of Western enterprises operating in the underdeveloped countries are faced with legislative restrictions on transfers, they know very well how to manipulate things so that their profits surface outside the country in which the investment is located: on the one hand, the price of raw materials exported to the parent company or another of its subsidiaries is held down; on the other, the price of the equipment or materials imported from the said parent company or fellow subsidiary is forced up.[18] It is also necessary to take into account the intervention of the big houses which specialize in international trade, for whom the profits—for instance, when such a company sells fifty thousand tons of Brazilian sugar to Morocco—accrue directly to London, New York, or Paris.

The spoils extracted from the peoples of the Third World through the deterioration of their terms of trade were estimated in Chapter IV, Section 4, at $4.5 billion in 1965, and it was explained why this sum should be added to the $6 billion of financial tribute analyzed here. A further sum of approximately $1.35 billion should be added for the receipts from the maritime shipping of Third World goods by the vessels of the developed capitalist countries (see Chapter V, Section 5).

As far as can be determined, the total drain on the Third World by the imperialist countries came to some $12 billion in 1964–65—that is, 1.5 times the total volume of aid. So it is not the imperialist countries which aid the Third World, but the Third World which aids imperialism.

This pedestrian arithmetical calculation has the sole purpose of exposing the myth of aid, and it is clear that it is quite powerless to give a real idea of the enrichment imperialism derives from the pillage of the Third World. To do this it would be necessary to measure the enormous value added to the irreplaceable raw materials of the Third World by their industrial conversion in the developed countries. This added value is not, certainly, the sole achievement of the Third World, but would be impossible without its contribution.

To return to the much vaunted aid, limited and illusory though it is, Table VI-7A gives some idea of the part played by its repay-

---

[18] In dealing with an entirely different problem, Octave Gélinier, deputy director of the General Council for Scientific Organization, touched on this in a debate in *Le Monde* of March 20, 1967. He showed the "volatility" of profit from international enterprises situated in the industrial European countries. As a prototype of organizations whose profits can easily come to light elsewhere, he cited the General Motors factory in Strasbourg. If it is not too difficult for profits to by-pass the frontiers of strongly administered and controlled nations, what freedom of movement they must have in the Third World countries, which are almost all insufficiently administered.

ments in the accounts of the Third World countries. Part B covers the unpaid portion of loans effectively contracted which, in 1965, rose to about 25 percent of the total public or guaranteed debt.

In its 1965–66 annual report, the World Bank stated that the developing countries have to make payments for the service of their public or guaranteed debt which "rose very sharply in 1964 and continued to rise in 1965." Thus, for the Third World—excluding Southern Europe—payments for the servicing of their debt have risen from an average of $2.1 billion for 1960–63 to $2.9 billion in 1964 and to $3.1 billion in 1965. Since public aid increased particularly rapidly for Latin America, it is natural that the cost of servicing the public debt also rose most rapidly for this region, and by 1965 was absorbing about one-sixth of receipts from exports. In 1964–65 the cost of servicing the debts of all the developed countries together was as much, or even more, than 9 percent of their receipts from exported goods.

By December 31, 1965, the total public and guaranteed debt of the Third World countries came to the enormous sum of $32.7 billion (see Table VI-7B). This was more than eleven times the net total of bi- and multilateral loans received in 1965 ($2.9 billion).

It might be of interest to try to compare the cost of servicing the debt with the gross total of new public loans made to the Third World by the rich capitalist countries—this time not adjusting for capital repayments. In view of what has been said above, it can be estimated that in 1965 the interest on loans on the one hand and on export credit guarantees on the other, must be of the order of $550 million and $600 million respectively—a total of $1,150 million. The portion of the servicing of the public or guaranteed debt of the Third World devoted to capital repayments comes to: $3,100 million − $1,150 million = $1,950 million. For the same year, the gross total of new public loans stood at about: $2,900 million + $1,950 million = $4,850 million. Comparing this figure with that for the cost of servicing the public and guaranteed debt in 1965 ($3,100 million) shows that some 64 percent of all new bi- or multilateral public loans are absorbed simply in the servicing of the public debt. In other words, new public loans to the Third World served mainly to service and repay accumulated old debts. This was confirmed by George D. Woods, president of the World Bank, in his address to the World Monetary Conference in Rio de Janeiro on September 26, 1966: "The servicing of official debts from the past (including interest and amortization) already cancels out some two-thirds of the official movement of capital into the developing countries." Mr. Woods added that if things remain unchanged, "development aid will purely and simply consume itself."

The accumulation of debt is accentuated by the fact that often, owing to the circumstances set out earlier, Third World countries are unable to pay their dues on time and are driven to ask for moratoria. The United Nations Conference for Trade and Development (Geneva, 1964) recommended that in such cases the creditor nations should cooperate to reach agreements entailing "the renegotiation or consolidation of the debt with appropriate periods of grace and terms for amortization and reasonable rates of interest." Thus Indonesia, who was being punished for her anti-imperialist stance when, in 1964, she was only accorded public aid amounting to half the average for the previous three years, became the object of the utmost solicitude on the part of the ten Western countries after the massacre of Indonesian Communists. Meetings took place all during the last six months of 1966 and by the end of December an agreement was reached consolidating part of the Indonesian external debt and fixing another meeting in 1967 to consider whether further relief would be opportune; this meeting was to be preceded by one between the creditor nations and international institutions to study what aid might in future be given to Indonesian programs for stabilization and reconstruction.[19]

Apart from the case of Indonesia (to which we may add that of Ghana), is there any reason to expect a general alleviation of the terms on which public aid is available to the Third World countries? First, no one in authority expects it to increase in volume. George D. Woods, in his speech of September 26, 1966, declared that "assistance from public sources is not increasing; for the fifth year in succession it has fallen as a proportion of the revenue of

---

[19] *Le Monde,* December 22, 1966.

the industrialized countries." The 1965–66 World Bank annual report (p. 35) considers that "on the whole, official assistance has tended to become less rather than more concessionary, because of the decline in the share of grants and grant-like contributions (such as long-term credits repayable in local currencies) in the total official bilateral capital flow—from 70 percent in 1960 to 52 percent in 1965—and that "the average interest rate on bilateral loan commitments increased from 3 percent in 1964 to 3.6 percent in 1965 and average maturities shortened from 28.3 years to 22.1 years." The 1966 figures show a further decline of Western aid expressed as a percentage of the national revenue of the DAC countries.

While the total public aid to the Third World is bound to decline, or at best remain stable in relative value, the charge on this aid included in the public debt must rise, both because of the increase in loans as opposed to gifts and because of higher interest rates and shorter periods of repayment. The Third World countries will be tied ever more closely to a form of public aid which brings only what is necessary to pay for earlier aid while, taking one year with another, private aid pumps out of the Third World a little more than three times what it puts in. The Indonesian experience is only the bloodiest and most striking example of the political subjection that goes along with the financial subjection that is slowly draining away the meager subsistance of the proletarian nations.

What purpose does all this serve? According to Paul-Marc Henry, deputy director of the United Nations Development Program: "The subsidies and other payments paid by the industrial nations benefit only a tiny fraction of the populations concerned, usually the fraction that is least in need of aid. The rest is either wasted or spent on the working of the clumsy apparatus for its own distribution, or misappropriated by the well-to-do."[20]

---

[20] *Le Monde,* March 2, 1967.

Table VI-1

Assistance to the Third World:
Total Net Value of All Forms of Assistance to the
Less Developed Countries* from 1960 to 1965
(in millions of $U.S.)

	1960	1963	1964	1965
I — Public bilateral sector, net	4,317	5,712	5,441	5,773
a) Gifts and assimilated contributions		4,040	3,836	3,798
of which: technical assistance		(858)	(950)	(1,048)
reparations and indemnities		(140)	(126)	(141)
loans reimbursable in local currency		(306)	(229)	(130)
sales payable in local currency		(999)	(1,056)	(810)
b) Long-term loans, net		1,673	1,604	1,975
II — Public multilateral sector, net	671	411	441	498
III — Private investments and loans, net		1,838	2,318	3,138
a) Direct new investments		1,011	970	1,371
b) Reinvested profits		620	743	836
c) Portfolio investments		206	605	931
	2,958			
IV — Private export credits for more than one year, net				
guaranteed		487	777	646
not guaranteed		65	104	95
Total		552	881	741
Total for CAD countries**	**7,947**	**8,513**	**9,081**	**10,150**
Estimated total of contributions from non-member countries	360	647	662	675
Additional multilateral contributions, net***	−604	+256	+195	+131
Total received by the underdeveloped countries	**7,703**	**9,416**	**9,938**	**10,956**

*These countries include, apart from the Third World, the following European countries: Spain, Greece, Yugoslavia, Malta, Cyprus, and Gibraltar, as well as Israel.

**These are: United States, Canada, Austria, Belgium, Denmark, France, West Germany, Italy, Netherlands, Portugal, Sweden, Great Britain, Japan, and Australia.

***Difference between the payments affected by the multilateral organizations and their receipts during the year, including countries not members of the CAD.

Source: Development Assistance Efforts and Policies, OECD, 1966 Review, Tables II, 5, 6, and 7.

Table VI-2

Aid from the Advanced Capitalist Countries to the Third World

A. Composition

> **38**/40 % in public bilateral gifts;
> 24/25 % in public bilateral loans;
> 28/30 % in private investments;
> 7/8   % in multilateral aid.

B. The Principal Countries Providing Aid in 1964-65

United States	53-55% of the total
France	13-15% "
United Kingdom	9-10% "
West Germany	7% "
Japan	3-5% "

Source: Figures extracted by the author from various documents.

Table VI-3

**Geographical Distribution of the Financial
Resources Placed at the Disposal of the Third World
and the Less Developed Countries (1960-1964)
(in millions of $U.S.)**

	Net bilateral public funds		Net multilateral funds		Private export credit guarantee*	
	1960	1964	1960	1964	1960	1964
Southern Europe and Israel	**491**	**414**	**− 8**	**48**	**116**	**164**
Latin America	**278**	**676**	**11**	**314**	**276**	**86**
% of total**	8%	14%	4%	44%	72%	13%
North of the Sahara	709	645	89	28	6	113
South of the Sahara	615	932	69	157	58	193
Total Africa	**1,324**	**1,577**	**158**	**186**	**64**	**306**
% of total**	35%	32%	54%	26%	17%	46%
Middle East, except Israel	149	98	29	37	48	− 32
South Asia	1,059	1,712	63	123	− 71	115
Far East	830	725	9	43	70	179
Total Asia	**2,038**	**2,535**	**101**	**203**	**47**	**262**
% of total**	54%	51%	35%	28%	12%	40%
Oceania and others	**142**	**192**	**20**	**13**	**− 5**	**5**
Totals	**4,272**	**5,392**	**282**	**764**	**498**	**823**

*Net variation. Israel is included in the Middle East.
**Southern Europe is excluded from the total.

*Source: Geographical Distribution of Financial Flows to Less-Developed Countries, 1960-
1964, OECD, various tables.*

Table VI-4

Direct Private United States Investments Abroad and Value and Profits Repatriated
(in millions of dollars)

	Direct Accumulated Investments as of December 31										Profits Repatriated Annually							
	1960	1962	1963	Total	1964 (preliminary)						1960	1962	1963	Total	1964 (preliminary)			
					Mining & Smelting	Petrol-eum	Manuf.	Public Utilities	Trade	Other					Mining & Smelt.	Petrol-eum	Manuf.	Other
All areas	**32,778**	**37,226**	**40,686**	**44,343**	**3,564** (8%)	**14,350** (32.4%)	**16,861** (38%)	**2,023** (4.6%)	**3,736** (8.4%)	**3,808**	**2,355**	**3,050**	**3,134**	**3,471**	**399**	**1,922**	**876**	**543**
Canada	11,198	12,133	13,044	13,820	1,671	3,228	6,191	467	805	1,458	361	476	455	634	114	118	269	133
Europe	6,681	8,930	10,340	12,067	56	3,086	6,547	53	1,472	854	397	526	507	654	5	64	412	173
Oceania[1]	994	1,271	1,460	1,582	100	444	856	2	87	93	37	75	57	59	3	-6	53	10
Whole group	**18,873**	**22,334**	**24,844**	**27,469**	**1,827** (6.6%)	**6,758** (24.6%)	**13,594** (49.5%)	**522** (1.9%)	**2,364** (8.7%)	**2,405** (8.7%)	**795**	**1,077**	**1,019**	**1,347**	**122**	**176**	**734**	**316**
Latin America	8,387	8,424	8,662	8,932	1,098[4]	3,142[5]	2,340	568	951	832	641	761	801	900	172[4]	503[5]	92	133
Other Western hemisphere	884	1,050	1,229	1,386	250	569	166	49	89	263	78	130	155	116	73	33	4	7
Africa	925	1,271	1,426	1,629	356	830	225	2	93	122	-17	34	123	301	32	223	13	34
Asia[2]	2,291	2,500	2,793	3,062	34	2,014	535	55	238	186	853	1,017	1,017	1,046	1	960	34	50
Whole group	**12,487**	**13,245**	**14,110**	**15,009**	**1,738** (11.6%)	**6,555** (43.7%)	**3,266** (21.7%)	**674** (4.5%)	**1,371** (9.1%)	**1,403** (9.3%)	**1,555**	**1,942**	**2,096**	**2,363**	**278**	**1,719**	**143**	**224**
International[3]	1,418	1,647	1,733	1,865	–	1,038	–	827	–	–	5	32	19	30	–	26	–	4

[1] Australia = about 9/10 of this.
[2] Apparently includes Japan and Israel.
[3] Includes shipping enterprises registered in Liberia and Panama but operating worldwide.
[4] The figures for Argentina, Colombia and Chile are included in the heading "Others."
[5] The figures for Argentina and Chile are included in the heading "Others."

Source: *Statistical Abstract of the United States, 1966, Table 1239.*

124

Table VI-5

Returns on Foreign Investments Transferred
by the Third World Countries in 1964*
(in millions of $U.S.)

Argentina	103	Iran	456
Brazil	189	Iraq	331
Chile	106	Saudi Arabia	370
Colombia	73	U.A.R.	18
Mexico	324	Turkey	42
Peru	72	**Total for these Middle East**	
Puerto Rico	212	**countries**	**1,217**
Venezuela	653	India	211
Other Latin American countries	238	Malaysia	67
Total Latin America	**1,970**	Pakistan	55
		Philippines	25
Ghana	18	Others, not including certain	
Ivory Coast	25	countries (notably Indonesia)	19
Libya	200	**Total (incomplete) for South**	
Nigeria	69	**and East Asia**	**377**
Rhodesia	54		
Zambia	97	**Recapitulation**	
South Africa	235		
Others, not including certain		Latin America	1,970
countries (notably Congo-		Africa	748
Kinshasa)	50	Middle East	1,217
Total (incomplete) for Africa	**748**	South and East Asia	377
		Total Third World, excepting	
		certain countries	4,312
		Est. total of all the Third World	4,900

*The revenues shown include: revenues for direct investments, other dividends and various returns.

Source: Balance of Payments Yearbook, IMF, Volume 17, 1960-1964, Table "Summary Balance of Payments Statements," Column "Investment Income."

Table VI-6

A. Final Balance on Transferred Revenues for Several Advanced Capitalist Countries
(in millions of $ U.S.)

United States and Canada	+ 4,439
Western Europe	+ 1,044
Japan	− 196
Australia and New Zealand	− 328
Israel	− 54
Net total	+ 4,905

Source: Figures calculated by the author.

B. Amortization and Interest on Loans to the Third World
(in millions of $U.S.)

		Interest	
	Amortization	C.A.D. countries	Of which U.S.A.:
1962	423	294	
1963	489	316	172
1964	699	421	239
1965	767	458	233

Source: Development Assistance Efforts and Policies, OECD, 1966 Review, Tables IX, 5, 6, and 7.

C. Third World Loss in the Form of Dividends and Private Profits Together with Interest, Loans, and Credits, 1964
(in millions of $ U.S.)

Total of dividends and private repatriated revenue	4,900
Interest from bi- and multilateral private loans	500
Interest on export credits	600
	6,000

Source: Figures calculated by the author.

Table VI-7

A. Payments Made to Service the External Public or State Guaranteed Debt of 97 Developing Countries (estimates in billions of $U.S.)

	Latin America	South Asia and Middle East	Far East	Africa	Southern Europe	Total	Total without Southern Europe	Total as % of merchandise exports
1960	1.4	0.4	0.1	0.1	0.3	2.3	2.0	8.1%
1961	1.3	0.4	0.2	0.1	0.3	2.3	2.0	8.2%
1962	1.3	0.5	0.3	0.1	0.2	2.5	2.3	8.4%
1963	1.3	0.5	0.2	0.2	0.3	2.4	2.1	7.5%
1964	1.7	0.7	0.2	0.3	0.4	3.3	2.9	9.2%
1965	1.7	0.8	0.3	0.3	0.4	3.5	3.1	9.0%

B. Total External Public or State Guaranteed Debt Not Amortized (Including Undisbursed) of 97 Developing Countries as of December 31, 1965 (in billions of $U.S.)

	Disbursed	Undisbursed	Total
Latin America	9.4	2.5	11.9
South Asia and Middle East	8.5	2.8	11.3
Far East	2.5	2.0	4.5
Africa	4.0	1.0	5.0
Southern Europe	2.9	0.8	3.7
Total of above areas	**27.3**	**9.1**	**36.4**
Total without Southern Europe	**24.4**	**8.3**	**32.7**

Sources: World Bank and IDA Annual Report, 1965-66, Tables 3 and 4.

Chapter VII

Prospects

Confronted by a capitalist world in the throes of its second industrial revolution, and a socialist world which, in spite of errors and hesitations, is growing economically faster than any other, the Third World is stagnating or regressing. The underdeveloped half of the world has the highest rate of population growth, yet has less than 12 percent of the world's gross product, and the per capita increase in wealth is slower there than in other parts of the world.

The agricultural products required for the subsistence of the peoples of the Third World are not increasing as fast as the population; undernourishment and malnutrition rage in Asia, Africa, and Latin America; famine threatens; and the future is even darker than the present. At the time of automation and electronics in the West, the industrial production of the Third World does not reach 7 percent of the world total and its industrialization is proceeding at a slower per capita rate than the already industrialized countries. On the other hand, the agricultural products of the Third World destined for the factories or consumer markets of the rich capitalist countries are developing at a very satisfactory rate, and its mineral production, which goes largely to supplying the conversion industries of the developed countries, forms an increasingly important—and often determining—proportion of the total supply of raw materials and energy.

The backwardness of the Third World has certainly not generally been created by colonialism and imperialism; it existed before them and, indeed, made colonial conquest and subjection possible. But it is undeniable that it is the international division

129

of labor characteristic of imperialism which perpetuates the underdevelopment of the backward nations of Asia, Africa, and
Latin America, and condemns them to be purveyors of basic
foodstuffs, raw materials, and crude oil to the dominant nations
which reserve for themselves that industrialization which multi-
plies wealth. Thus half the world grows in its soil and extracts
from beneath it the most possible, only to meet the needs of that
fifth of the world which holds it in subjection.

Political decolonization has done nothing to alter the system of
pillage. Change has no more come to pass in Africa and Asia than
it has in Latin America, where national governments have had
the appearance of power for 150 years. In newly independent
countries, imperialism has almost always been able to conciliate
leading groups subservient to it or willing to become so under
pressure. Whether it rules directly or through intermediaries, the
result remains the same, except that an awareness has begun to
develop and it has become necessary to contrive certain deceptions.

The most important of these takes the form of aid from the rich
to the poor countries. The latter must be led to believe that the
former are full of good intentions toward them, and the United
Nations has set out to make the years 1960 to 1970 a development decade. But imperialism cannot act contrary to its nature,
and its aid is deformed by all the defects inherent in the capitalist
system. More than half way through the great decade, not only
does the objective of bringing aid at least to the level of 1 percent
of the accumulated national income of the countries giving it
remain far from fulfillment, but the president of the World Bank
and many others have been obliged to admit that it is in reality
further away than before. Criticism of the effectiveness of this
aid is constantly becoming sharper and more insistent; such criticism is expressed even in the most official quarters.

This aid does not appear to be any compensation for, or a
partial redistribution of, the wealth pillaged from the underdeveloped world. On the contrary, it has been integrated into the
process of pillage and is, in present circumstances, an essential
part of the machinery. Its appearance is designed to deceive the
peoples of the Third World as well as those of the rich countries
who ultimately pay for it. This gives rise to the "publicity poster"

style in which it is conducted. Its true nature, its real character, however, is that of an indispensable aid to monopoly capitalism. On the one hand, it perpetuates the political corruption of almost all the leaders of the countries receiving aid, serving to keep these countries within the imperialist orbit inside which capital can thrive. On the other hand, since business is business and the appetite for profit insatiable, the aid itself brings preferential positions and opens or enlarges markets which the imperialist rivals fight for by an auction in export credits. Bilateral aid with strings attached or international aid plays this role as does the private investment which yearly drains from the Third World three times as much capital as it puts into it. Sometimes the hunt is in private preserves, sometimes the spoils are shared, but pillage it remains.

In these circumstances, how can it be suggested that the peoples of the Third World can rise from their underdevelopment without first breaking the chains of imperialism? What desperate self-deception could make anyone believe that imperialism could ascend to, or even promote, the economic emancipation of the countries whose exploitation is a condition of its own survival? This is the key to the problem: imperialism does not pillage the Third World diabolically or for fun, but because of *vital necessity,* because it could not survive otherwise. Appearances to the contrary, this is especially true of American super-imperialism, and it is not by coincidence that it both seeks economic domination over the world it calls free and sets itself up in the role of policeman. It may be difficult, if not impossible, to unravel the skein of American economic and financial interests throughout the world. However, Harry Magdoff provides some valuable clues. Instead of comparing United States exports with the gross national product—a comparison without significance because GNP includes government spending, services, commerce, and the transactions of banks, real estate companies, and stockbrokers—he compares the value of exports with the value of total internal production of moveable goods: agricultural products, minerals, manufactures, and shipping. To the value of exports produced in the United States, he adds the value of production abroad engendered by American investment, and thus expresses the importance in dollars of the sum total of foreign markets for United States enterprises, from United States firms operating at home and abroad. In 1964 this extended value of foreign markets absorbing United States exports came to two-fifths of the total value of American internal production of agricultural goods, manufactures, and minerals. This demonstrates the enormous importance of the world market to the economy of the United States and helps explain the American urge to dominate it at all costs.

The Third World does not, of course, appear separately in these calculations. But it may be recalled that this Third World absorbs more or less one-third of American exports and a similar proportion of direct American investments, and it should be emphasized that many United States enterprises in other industrialized countries themselves export to the Third World and thus act as relay stations. It appears quite certain that the underdeveloped countries of Asia, Africa, and Latin America play an important role (unfortunately it is difficult to assess, but is doubtless of the order of 15 to 18 percent) with regard to United States production of moveable goods.

We have indicated elsewhere that the exports of manufactured goods from all the industrialized countries to the Third World make up some 6 percent of their total manufacturing production and, while this is not a negligible proportion, we expressed the view that such exports do not constitute the main link of dependence tying the developed countries to the Third World. The most important link lay in the field of raw materials.

We only return to this subject to quote a passage from someone with views quite different from our own, namely President Eisenhower. Harry Magdoff quotes as follows from Eisenhower's inaugural address of January 20, 1953: "We know . . . that we are linked to all free peoples not merely by a noble idea but by a simple need. No free people can for long cling to any privilege or enjoy any safety in economic solitude. For all our own material might, even we need markets in the world for the surpluses of our farms and our factories. Equally, we need for the same farms and factories vital materials and products of distant lands." The last words of this unadorned confession undoubtedly refer to the underdeveloped countries of the Third World. Harry Magdoff comments most justly: "Quite understandably the government makes its contribution to the security of the nation as well as to the security of business . . . , and last but not least a foreign aid program which is a fine blend of declared humanitarian aims about industrialization and a realistic appreciation that such progress should not interfere with the ability of the supplying countries to maintain a proper flow of raw materials."[1] Clarence B. Randall, president of Inland Steel and adviser to Washington on foreign aid, is also quoted by Harry Magdoff. Referring to the fortunate conjunction of events which enabled the United States to make use of the uranium deposits in the ex-Belgian Congo when manufacturing atomic bombs, Randall said: "What a break it was for us that the mother country was on our side! And who can possibly foresee today which of the vast unexplored areas of the world may likewise possess some unique deposit of a rare raw material which in the fullness of time our industry or our defense program may most urgently need?"[2] Harry Magdoff adds a final comment: "The integration of less developed capitalisms into the world market as reliable and continuous suppliers of their natural resources results, with rare exceptions, in a continuous dependency on the centers of monopoly control. . . ."

This dependence and control cannot co-exist with the economic autonomy of the Third World countries, nor with development based on the full utilization of their national resources since imperialism must maintain a complete, permanent, and stable hold over these resources, and especially over raw materials, whether they are already discovered and exploited or still to be found. Imperialism takes possession of the latter in advance to provide for its future needs. And yet plans of all kinds proliferate, without any question of ending this dependence and control, pretending to map out the development of the Third World within the framework of the present system. These plans often contain ideas which would be good if imperialism were not imperialism. However, if it remains what it has always been, if its urge to dominate the world market remains as strong as before—if not stronger—then it must be admitted that, however pure their motives, the authors of such

---

[1] Magdoff, *op. cit.*, pp. 196–97.
[2] *Ibid.*, p. 197.

plans and models are objectively aiding imperialism by fostering the illusion that it is not an insurmountable obstacle to development. For us, the time for development plans and models has not yet come. Of course we can think ahead, but always from a different viewpoint[3] and not without posing the breaking of imperialist chains as an essential precondition. The struggle for emancipation takes precedence over construction, which in turn cannot occur without it.

In 1963, eighteen African states and Madagascar associated themselves with the six countries of the Common Market, believing perhaps that this would give them improved opportunities to benefit from their own wealth. A whole chapter of my previous book was devoted to an analysis of the convention of association, which appeared to me to provide the framework for a new-style EEC imperialism, operated through cooperatives and stock-holding companies. Thus the subsequent disillusionment of the African signatories came as no surprise. Diori Hamani, president of Niger, expressed this disappointment:[4]

> For our part, we, the African states, have loyally implemented the Yaoundé Convention. But, on the European side, we notice more and more: (1) That bilateral aid to our countries is decreasing or, at best, stagnating; (2) that the prices of our agricultural products are steadily declining; (3) that the prices of industrial products continue to rise.
>
> Moreover, several of the Six have imposed taxes on the products we export to them.

The same feeling was expressed by M. Zinzou, foreign minister of Dahomey, who echoed the criticisms formulated once again by Diori Hamani.[5] And, taking the Ivory Coast as an example, Phillipe Decraene reported that "between 1963 and 1965 exports from the Ivory Coast to the EEC countries only grew in value by 6 percent, while the value of imports from these same countries increased by 36 percent. In this respect at least, the convention of

---

[3] This was done very well by Charles Bettelheim in *Planification et Croissance accélérée, op. cit.,* Chapter 4.
[4] *Le Monde,* November 1, 1966.
[5] *Le Monde,* December 13, 1966.

association of the eighteen African countries and the Six of the Common Market has been more profitable for the latter." M. Decraene added:

> The index of the unit value of Ivory Coast exports to the EEC countries fell from 100 in 1960 to 74 in 1964 while the index of the unit value of its imports from the EEC countries rose from 100 to 123 during the same period.
>
> It is estimated in Abidjan that the purchasing power derived from the export of the Ivory Coast's traditional products—coffee, cocoa, and bananas—fell by 26 percent annually between 1961 and 1964. In absolute value, the fall in the purchasing power of these exports was of the order of $281 million between 1961 and 1965. By December 31, 1965, the total aid given to the Ivory Coast by the Fund for Aid and Cooperation (France) and the European Development Fund (EDF) amounted to only $58,708,000. Thus aid made up for only one-fifth of the loss which had been suffered.[6]

The author adds that only a few days earlier the EEC had agreed to pay Italy $140 million "to compensate it for the difference between the price of its olive oil and that offered on the world market."

This shows who is helping whom. Even to the most submissive Third World leaders, imperialism can offer only fraudulent contracts which perpetuate and aggravate its domination. Doubtless, however, development of some Third World countries has actually improved in recent years and this is, of course, cited as proof of what might be possible. The Ivory Coast is precisely one of those which has been used for propaganda purposes and has been said to be enjoying an economic miracle. But we have shown that agricultural expansion, as long as the country remains in the imperialist orbit producing for the markets of the rich capitalist countries, does not allow sufficient primitive accumulation to provide the foundation for autonomous industrialization. It follows that the first steps toward industrialization in the Ivory Coast depend upon foreign capital, which is in the first place irrelevant to the economic autonomy of the country, because it constitutes highly and rapidly profitable enclaves which are themselves geared to the

---

[6] *Le Monde,* June 1–2, 1967.

imperialist world market; and in the second place, as we saw in the preceding chapter, in the long run creates an endless leakage of currency through the transfer of their dividends. Phases of expansion may occur and look like leading to the economic take-off stage, but these will be no more than false starts which cannot create the continuous accumulation which is indispensable to balanced and lasting development.

Mexico is also often cited as a country which is alleged to have achieved "economic take-off," and one whose gross internal product rose (in absolute value at constant prices) on an average of 5.6 percent per annum from 1958 to 1965 and of 2.2 percent per annum per head. While this is no miracle, it is encouraging progress. However, the Mexican economy has, to a large extent, continued to be of the "dualist" type, and 55 percent of the active population is engaged in agriculture. Mexico's balance of trade is persistently and considerably unfavorable. Moreover, and this point always recurs, the burden of external debt is very heavy (unamortized debt of $2.1 billion, average interest rate of over 6 percent). Even more significant is the fact that foreign investments, nine-tenths of which are American, alone caused revenue transfers of $324 million in 1964 (see Table VI-5)—that is, 31 percent of the value of exports for the same year—while the value of exports was in turn $422 million less than that of imports (see Table V-3). So the prognosis is very doubtful. In certain special cases imperialism, especially United States imperialism, can hold up certain economies over which it has strong control in order to avoid "subversion" on its boundaries. But let us not talk of this as autonomous and balanced development or as economic take-off.[7]

In the last part of his book, Paul Bairoch concludes an analysis of the development possibilities of the non-Communist underdeveloped countries as follows: "The diagnosis is generally decidedly pessimistic; the effects of the beginnings of industrialization are being wiped out or compromised by the stagnation or even

---

[7] In Africa, the Cameroons are cited and in Latin America, Venezuela. The latter has a per capita gross internal product on the order of $1,000. Yet in *Le Monde* (March 19–22, 1966), Anne Philippe entitled her investigation of that country: "Venezuela: A Rich Country but a Poor People."

regression of agriculture." He goes on to say that the Third World "has made a bad start and the chances of an early take-off are very slight." He continues: "On the other hand, China seems to have reached the point of economic take-off." He notes that there is a considerable divergence between the Chinese statistics and the more conservative estimates of Western experts, but goes on: "It seems true that China has succeeded in reaching economic take-off even if the diagnosis is based on Western data, and this success seems all the more brilliant by contrast with the non-Communist underdeveloped world."[8] Chinese per capita income has been growing at an increasing rate and "since about 1955 it has bypassed that of the rest of Asia, to which it was inferior in 1950. Today it is 40 percent higher . . . using Western estimates." The author asks himself "what lies behind such great divergence" and concludes that "the Chinese system is very likely the basis of the economic success achieved in that country but it is not certain that it would be as successful if applied to other societies."

None will dispute this last point and Charles Bettelheim and Jacques Charrière, who are far from Paul Bairoch on many issues, agree that "there cannot be a 'model' for the construction of socialism which can really be transferred from one country to another," adding that "each experiment in socialist construction is, however, a source of very valuable lessons for other countries that are also setting out on the road to socialism."[9] And they suggest in their introduction that "the two facts that China is the first to have gone over to socialism from such a low industrial level, and that the Chinese revolution in the countryside is an example of agrarian success remarkable among the socialist countries, are rich in lessons for the non-industrialized countries."

Paul Bairoch's conclusions seem particularly interesting because the very least that can be said is that he seems uncommitted, since he insists that he is a pure economist for whom economy cannot be political. However, for this very reason his conclusions seem to our eyes inadequate, because in every case they stop at the point at which the imperialist system and the process of pillaging

---

[8] Bairoch, *op. cit.*

[9] Bettelheim and Charrière, *La construction du socialisme en Chine* (Paris: François Maspero, 1965).

the Third World must be challeneged. If China has succeeded where India—often counterposed—has failed, it is fundamentally because China broke all links with imperialism and India preserved them. And, it must be repeated, all socialist construction is impossible until such links are broken. For this reason, whatever efforts Guinea or Algeria can or will make, they cannot be —or become—socialist countries in their present circumstances.

The absolute priority of the anti-imperialist struggle is shown on every page of a remarkable book written by A.-P. Lentin on his return from the Tricontinental Conference held in Havana in January 1966.[10] Three of the four parts of this basic book are entitled: "Imperialism Today," "The Anti-Imperialist Struggle," and "Anti-Imperialist Solidarity," in the order in which these subjects are found in the final resolution prepared by the Economic Commission of the Tricontinental Conference. The resolution, after denouncing imperialism in the preamble, set out a nine-point proclamation. The first point states the "principle of the elimination of the exploitation of man by man through non-capitalist development leading to socialism"; the second point declares that the common struggle to eliminate imperialism is an absolute necessity; and the third point stresses the active solidarity of the peoples of the three continents. The real Third World is that of the revolutionary peoples and organizations and not that of bought leaders, and that Third World has made a good start.

A good start for a Third World in this sense does not unfortunately mean that the goal is near, and A.-P. Lentin is right to call his last chapter "The Long March." In this chapter he assesses the perspectives for the total liberation of the peoples of the Third World, but for him, as for us, the end is not in doubt.

The Central Committee of the Chinese Communist Party was equally correct when it wrote in a twenty-five point letter in June 1963 that "it is in the vast regions of Africa, Asia, and Latin America that the various contradictions of the contemporary world converge, that imperialist domination is weakest, and these regions are the storm center where the world revolution is making a direct assault upon imperialism." The phrase "imperialist domination

---

[10] A.-P. Lentin, *La lutte tricontinentale* (Paris: François Maspero, 1966).

is weakest" may at first sight seem irreconcilable with the picture we have presented of fierce imperialist exploitation of the Third World, but there is no philosophical contradiction here. From the moment when the people's consciousness is awakened— and the Tricontinental Conference has given us proof of that— it will be natural for imperialism to be opposed most strongly where its oppression is severest. An anti-imperialist war is raging not in the West, but in Vietnam; guerrillas are rising in the cordilleras of South America, not in the mountains of France; imperialism has had to shed oceans of blood to gain a respite for itself in Santo Domingo and Indonesia, not in Britain or Switzerland. The anti-imperialist storm is brewing in Africa, not in Europe.

The march of the Third World peoples to their total emancipation will be as hard as it will be long. Imperialism knows that its own survival is at stake, even in our Western world which appears to be so calm. We hope we have shown that imperialism's life blood is drawn mainly from the raw materials of the Third World. This is not a new idea. Harry Magdoff writes:

> The economic control, and hence the political control when dealing with foreign sources of raw material supplies, is of paramount importance to the monopoly-organized mass production industries in the home country. In industries such as steel, aluminium, and oil, the ability to control the source of raw material is essential to the control over the markets and prices of the final products, and serves as an effective safety factor in protecting the large investment in the manufacture and distribution of the final product. . . . [Competitors] cannot live very long without a dependable source of raw materials at a practical cost. . . . these foreign supplies are not merely an avenue to great profits but are the insurance policy on the monopolistic position at home.[11]

Imperialism has geared the productive capacity of its factories to the needs of the world it calls free. Yet in some cases excess capacity has already appeared. The annual report of the British Iron and Steel Federation states that in 1966 surplus world steel production was 84 million tons and was equal to the production of the six Common Market countries. A front-page article in

---

[11] Magdoff, *op. cit.*, p. 195.

Figaro by Jean Lecerf, entitled "Steel Crisis—Explosion of the
Third World," is significant in this connection. "Steel is only part
of a vast problem: the eruption of the Third World into life. This
will push us into the most complex undertakings, bringing the
highest returns, but will also oblige us to abandon, however difficult, many techniques with a high labor content which can be
more suitably conducted by the new nations."[12] Yet the Third
World's intrusion into the iron and steel industry is still extremely
modest: in 1964 it produced only 4 percent of the world's steel—
6 percent excluding the socialist countries (see Table VI-4).
Even though Jean Lecerf's article makes some debatable statements (imperialism will not "abandon" steel any more than any-
thing else as the development of new steel works at ports indicates), it is interesting as an expression of anxiety at the idea of
the Third World breaking into industrialization, and it makes clear
the terrible difficulties that will result for imperialism.

When the natural resources, especially the minerals, of the
Third World come to be developed on any scale—by the Third
World itself and not by the industrialized capitalist countries—this
will certainly mean a crisis for imperialism which may well prove
insurmountable: it will be left with insufficient room to maneuver.
Deprived of the vast Third World, imperialism would become a
system in a "ghetto," which is quite inconceivable. We have shown,
repeated, and emphasized that the pillage of the Third World is
a vital need, a functional necessity, for imperialism. Harry Magdoff sees this pillage as the "life insurance" of the monopolies. To
go on from this to estimate how long imperialism can survive, or
imagine the form its death agony will take, would be to move
into the realm of prophecies. At most one can speculate that when
imperialism is confronted by the "terrible difficulties" forseen by
Jean Lecerf, these difficulties will place the proletariats of the
Western countries once more in a revolutionary perspective, and
perhaps under pressure from them the parties and organizations
which represent them may abandon their present reformism. It
appears that for their part, the delegates to the Tricontinental
Conference have not given up hope that this may happen. In the

---

[12] November 1, 1966.

preamble to their final economic resolution, they chose to affirm that their struggle for emancipation "is closely linked to the struggle of the working classes in the capitalist countries against the monopolies, and that close cooperation between these forces is of great importance for the defeat of imperialism."

However, it is beyond question that for the present "the various contradictions of the contemporary world converge" in the Third World, and it is there that imperialism faces, and will face, the most direct challenge. Today the anti-imperialist struggle of the peoples of Africa, Asia, and Latin America is decisive on a world scale; it will deprive imperialism of its economic living space, it will reanimate the revolutionary movements in those parts of the world where they are temporarily dormant. On April 16, 1967, the Organization for the Solidarity of the Peoples of Africa, Asia, and Latin America issued an admirable statement by Che Guevara: "Finally, it is necessary to take into account the fact that imperialism is a world system, the highest stage of capitalism, and that it must be defeated in a worldwide confrontation. The strategic purpose of this struggle must be the destruction of imperialism."

2

Descriptive Economic Indices
for Major Countries

These indices follow one another in the following order:

Socialist countries (six countries)
Developed capitalist countries (five countries)
African Third World (twenty-two countries)
Latin American Third World (thirteen countries)
Asian Third World (fifteen countries)

In each series the countries appear in alphabetical order.

The small number of indices for the countries of each of the first two groups is given for the sole purpose of providing terms of reference for the Third World countries. Moreover, as a general rule, our indices were established to facilitate comparisons. They give simple, sometimes even elementary, information, from which, however, the reader can very quickly form a rough but fair idea of the economy of the country concerned, and proceed from there to make comparisons.

Most of our figures are drawn from the different United Nations Yearbooks or from other international organizations. A few come from *Images économiques du monde, 1966*[1] and a few others from the tables appended to Paul Bairoch's book.[2] Some figures have been intentionally rounded off. Those concerning production are usually an approximate average of the results of the two or three most recent years. In the same way, the figures relating to the gross domestic product and especially to its average growth rate are, in certain cases, imprecise. In some cases, various equally official documents differed among themselves, and it became necessary to calculate approximate averages: these figures can only be regarded as orders of magnitude.

Since it was practically impossible to establish an index for

---

[1] Beaujeu-Garnier, *op. cit.*
[2] *Diagnostic de l'évolution économique du tiers monde 1900–1966, op. cit.*

145

each of the several hundred countries of the Third World, we gave preference to the most important and to some others which are in the news. Unfortunately, South Vietnam had to be omitted—as had North Vietnam from the list of socialist countries—since the imperialist war which ravages these two halves of a single country would make any figures we might produce useless, if not tragically derisory. And one of our greatest regrets is that there is no index for China, because of the absence of adequate recent data.

Finally two practical points:

1. "All industries" = Extractive and manufacturing industries taken together.

2. M. = Million.

Cuba

114,500 sq km.; 7,800,000 inhab. (+2.5% per year); 68 inhab. per sq. km.

Capital: Havana, 1,650,000 inhab. (conurbation).

Principal cities (more than 100,000 inhab.): Santiago de Cuba, Camagüey, Guantánamo, Santa Clara.

National currency: Peso = $1.00.

Gross domestic product in 1965 = 4,100 M. pesos (per capita = $540).

Annual growth rate 1958–65: 6 to 7%

Total budgetary expenditure in 1965: 2,535 M. pesos.

Per capita consumption in 1964: Energy: 931 kg; industrial steel: 29 kg.

Major products: Sugar: 6 M. tons (second biggest producer); tobacco: 60,000 tons; cigars: 600 M.; cigarettes: 18,000 M; cattle: 7.2 M. head; rice, cotton, citrus; manganese ore: 70,000 tons; chrome: 30,000 tons; cobalt, copper, nickel: 34,000 tons. Light industries (textiles, foodstuffs) which are developing; power stations, cement, fertilizers.

Foreign trade 1963, 1965

IMPORTS CIF 1963	M Pesos	EXPORTS FOB 1965	M Pesos
Food	197	Sugar	591
Crude materials, except fuel	37	Tobacco	32
Petroleum and products	80	Crude materials	25
Chemicals	81	Chemicals	26
Manufactured goods	154		
Machinery and transportation equipment	280		
Total	867	Total	685
PRINCIPAL SUPPLIERS 1963		**PRINCIPAL BUYERS 1965**	
U.S.S.R.	461	U.S.S.R.	322
China	91	China	100
Czechoslovakia	55	Czechoslovakia	45
		Spain	33

Czechoslovakia

128,000 sq. km.; 14.3 M. inhab. (+ 0.7% per year); 112 inhab. per sq. km.

Capital: Prague, 1.05 M. inhab.

Principal cities: Brno, 340,000; Bratislava, Ostrava, 270,000; Plzen, 150,000.

National currency: Koruna = $.139.

Net material product in 1965: 174 billion koruna. Agriculture: 13%; all industries: 65%.

Total budgetary expenditure in 1964: 130 billion koruna.

Per capita consumption in 1964: Energy: 5,789 kg; steel: 480 kg.

Major products: Wheat: 1.8 M. tons; barley: 1.4 M. tons; sugar: 1 M. tons; potatoes: 7.5 M. tons; hops; cattle: 4.5 M. head; pigs: 6 M. head; coal: 28 M. tons; lignite: 75 M. tons; antimony ore: 2,000 tons; iron, lead, and manganese ores; sulphur: 360,000 tons; radioactive minerals; steel: 8.5 million tons; cement: 5.6 M. tons; electricity: 34 billion kwhr; heavy industries, diverse light industries, paper: 500,000 tons; traditional industries: glass, porcelain, footwear, breweries.

Foreign trade 1965

IMPORTS FOB	M Korunas	EXPORTS FOB	M Korunas
Food	1,679	Food	573
Animal and vegetable raw materials	3,778	Animal and vegetable raw materials	1,211
Fuels, minerals, and metals	5,297	Fuels, minerals, and metals	3,937
Chemicals, fertilizers, rubber	1,462	Chemicals, fertilizers, rubber	732
Machinery and equipment	5,758	Machinery and equipment	9,385
Consumer goods of Industrial origin	1,006	Consumer goods of Industrial origin	3,194
Total	19,242	Total	19,357
PRINCIPAL SUPPLIERS		**PRINCIPAL BUYERS**	
U.S.S.R.	6,874	U.S.S.R.	7,364
East Germany	2,073	East Germany	1,995
Poland	1,502	Poland	1,791
Hungary	1,234	Hungary	952
Romania	679	West Germany	664
Bulgaria	642	Romania and Yugoslavia	497
West Germany	633		

East German Democratic Republic

108,300 sq. km.; 17,200,000 inhab.; 159 inhab. per sq. km.

Capital: Berlin, 1,100,000 inhab. (est).

Principal cities: Leipzig, 600,000 inhab.; Dresden, 510,000; Karl-Marx-Stadt, 290,000; Halle, 280,000; Magdeburg, 270,000.

National currency: East mark = $.45

Net material product in 1965: 83 billion marks. Agriculture: 13%; all industries: 74%.

Per capita consumption in 1964: Energy: 5,569 kg; industrial steel: 424 kg.

Major products: Potatoes: 13 M. tons; oats: 800,000 tons; rye: 1.9 M. tons (fourth largest producer); pigs: 9.5 M. head; sugar: 800,000 tons; lignite: 280 M. tons (largest producer); electricity: 53.5 billion kwhr; steel: 4.4 M. tons; cement: 6 M. tons; chemical industries, fertilizers, textile industries, mechanical products, optics (photographic), synthetic rubber: 95,000 tons.

Foreign trade 1965

IMPORTS FOB	M Marks	EXPORTS FOB	M Marks
(Statistics available only in volume)		(Statistics available only in volume)	
Total	11,769	Total	12,880
PRINCIPAL SUPPLIERS		PRINCIPAL BUYERS	
U.S.S.R.	5,064	U.S.S.R.	5,505
Czechoslovakia	1,103	Czechoslovakia	1,226
West Germany	1,075	West Germany	1,222
Poland	589	Poland	1,132
Hungary	521	Hungary	532
India	123	U.A.R.	129

Poland

312,500 sq. km.; 31.7 M. inhab. (+ 1.3% per year); 101 inhab. per sq. km.

Capital: Warsaw, 1.3 M. inhab.

Principal cities: Lodz, 760,000 inhab.; Lublin, 760,000; Kraców, 520,000; plus 20 cities of more than 100,000 inhab.

National currency: Zloty = $.25.

Net material product in 1965: 537 billion zloty. Agriculture: 23%; all industries: 51%.

Total budgetary expenditure in 1964: 274 billion zloty (1965: 289).

Per capita consumption in 1964: Energy: 3,518 kg; industrial steel: 265 kg.

Major products: Rye: 8 M. tons; oats: 2.5 M. tons; sugar: 1.7 M. tons; potatoes: 45 M. tons (second largest producer); coal: 120 M. tons (fifth largest producer); lignite: 22 M. tons; electricity: 44 billion kwhr; lead ore: 40,000 tons; zinc ore: 150,000 tons; sulphur: 240,000 tons; steel: 9 M. tons; cement: 9.5 M. tons; metallurgical, textile, and chemical industries.

Foreign trade 1965

IMPORTS FOB	M Zlotys	EXPORTS FOB	M Zlotys
Food	389	Food	1,306
Animal and vegetable raw materials	2,175	Animal and vegetable raw materials	714
Fuels, minerals, and metals	2,290	Fuels, minerals, and metals	2,237
Chemicals, fertilizers, rubber	748	Chemicals, fertilizers, rubber	339
Machinery and equipment	3,067	Machinery and equipment	3,069
Consumer goods of industrial origin	630	Consumer goods of industrial origin	1,096
Total	9,361	Total	8,911
PRINCIPAL SUPPLIERS		PRINCIPAL BUYERS	
U.S.S.R.	2,914	U.S.S.R.	3,125
East Germany	1,085	Czechoslovakia	834
Czechoslovakia	976	East Germany	613
Hungary	423	United Kingdom	510
United Kingdom	385	West Germany	451

Romania

237,500 sq. km.; 19,140,000 inhab. (+ 0.8% per year); 81
inhab. per sq. km.

Capital: Bucharest, 1.4 M. inhab. (conurbation).

Principal cities: Cluj, 180,000; Ploesti, Brasov, Iási: 140,000–
150,000; Constanta, Braila, Galati, Craiova, Arad, Sibiu,
Oradea: 120,000–130,000.

National currency: Leu = $.167.

Net material product: Agriculture: 30%; all industries: 48%.

Annual growth rate 1958–64: 9 to 10%.

Per capita consumption: Energy: 1,863 kg.; steel: 214 kg.

Major products: Wheat: 6 M. tons; maize: 6 M. tons; wood, fruit,
linen, hemp, cotton. Potatoes: 2.6 M. tons; sugar: 380,000
tons; cattle: 4.7 M. head; pigs: 6 M. head; sheep: 12.5 M.
head; crude oil: 12.5 M. tons; natural gas: 7 billion cubic
meters; coal: 6 M. tons; lignite: 6 M. tons; iron ore, manganese, silver; sulphur: 400,000 tons; cement: 5.4 M. tons;
steel: 3.4 M. tons; metallurgical, chemical, and textile industries.

Foreign trade 1965

IMPORTS FOB	M Lei	EXPORTS FOB	M Lei
Food	155	Food	919
Animal and vegetable raw materials	762	Animal and vegetable raw materials	1,420
Fuels, minerals and metals	2,090	Fuels, minerals and metals	1,667
Machinery and equipment	2,521	Machinery and equipment	1,223
Chemicals, fertilizers, rubber	407	Chemicals, fertilizers, rubber	425
Consumer goods of industrial origin	434	Consumer goods of industrial origin	728
Total	6,463	Total	6,609
PRINCIPAL SUPPLIERS		**PRINCIPAL BUYERS**	
U.S.S.R.	2,437	U.S.S.R.	2,631
West Germany	663	Czechoslovakia	571
Czechoslovakia	417	East Germany	430
East Germany	375	Italy	396
Italy	312	West Germany	380

U.S.S.R.

22,402,000 sq. km.; 1966: 233 M. inhab. (+ 1.6% per year); 10.4 inhab. per sq. km.

Capital: Moscow, 6.5 M. inhab.

Principal cities: Leningrad, 3.7 M.; Kiev, 1,330,000; Baku, 1,150,000; Gorki, Tashkent, Kharkov, 1,100,000; Novosibirsk, 1,050,000.

National currency: Ruble = $1.111.

Net material product in 1965: 192.6 billion rubles. Agriculture: 22%; all industries: 52%; construction: 9%.

Annual growth rate in 1965: 7 to 8%.

Total budgetary expenditure in 1965: 99,536 M. rubles.

Per capita consumption in 1964: Energy: 3,430 kg.; steel: 355 kg.

Major products: Wheat: 70 M. tons; sugar: 6.5 M. tons; potatoes: 70 M. tons (largest producer); cattle: 90 M. head; sheep: 140 M. head; pigs: 70 M. head; coal: 425 M. tons; crude oil: 243 M. tons; natural gas: 130 billion cubic meters; steel: 91 M. tons; cement: 75 M. tons; cotton thread: 1.3 M. tons; wool yarn: 240,000 tons; diversified heavy, light, and scientific industries.

Foreign trade 1965

IMPORTS FOB	M Roubles	EXPORTS FOB	M Roubles
Food, beverages, tobacco	1,491	Food, beverages	525
(of which: wheat)	(358)	Fuels and lubricants	1,265
(sugar)	(273)	Other raw materials	1,316
Fuels and lubricants	179	Machinery, transp. equip.	1,527
Other raw materials	898	Other manufactured goods	1,684
Machinery, transp. equip.	2,433	Other goods	1,038
Other manufactured goods	2,014		
Total	7,248	Total	7,350
PRINCIPAL SUPPLIERS		**PRINCIPAL BUYERS**	
European socialist countries	c. 4,300	European socialist countries	c. 4,100
Asian socialist countries	c. 300	Asian socialist countries	c. 400
European capitalist countries	c. 1,150	European capitalist countries	c. 1,500
Canada	c. 300	Canada	c. ?
Japan	c. 200	Japan	c. 200
Third World: Latin America	c. 400	Third World: Latin America	c. 450
Third World: Asia	c. 400	Third World: Asia	c. 400
Third World: Africa	c. 200	Third World: Africa	c. 250

France

551,000 sq. km.; 50 M. inhab. (+ 1.3% per year); 91 inhab. per
   sq. km.
Capital: Paris, 7.5 M. inhab. (conurbation).
Principal cities: Lyons, 900,000; Marseille, 830,000.
National currency: Franc = $0.204.
Gross national product in 1965: 470 billion francs = $94 billion
   ($1,920 dollars per inhab.). Agriculture: 8%; all industries
   and construction: 47%; services: 45%.
Annual growth rate 1955–65: 5%.
Total budgetary expenditure in 1964: 93.17 billion francs.
Per capita consumption in 1964: Energy: 2,933 kg.; steel: 356 kg.
Major products (1965): Cereals: 26.7 M. tons; wine: 60.5 M.
   hectoliters; cattle: 20.6 M. head; sheep and goats: 10 M.
   head; milk: 26.2 M. tons; coal: 51 M. tons; natural gas:
   5,100 M. cubic meters; iron ore: 20 M. tons; bauxite: 2.4
   M. tons; potassium: 2 M. tons; steel: 15.8 M. tons; cement:
   22.5 M. tons; automobiles: 1.4 M. units; all industries; balanced development of agriculture and industry.

Foreign trade 1965

IMPORTS CIF	M Francs	EXPORTS FOB	M Francs
Food, live animals, beverages, tobacco	8,749	Food, live animals, beverages, tobacco	7,895
Crude materials	7,752	Crude materials	3,536
Mineral fuels, lubricants, related materials	7,898	Mineral fuels, lubricants, related materials	1,608
Chemicals	3,487	Chemicals	5,007
Manufactured goods	9,124	Manufactured goods	13,764
Machinery, transp. materials	10,212	Machinery, transp. materials	13,045
Misc. manufactured goods	3,145	Misc. manufactured goods	4,139
Total	51,029	Total	49,608
PRINCIPAL SUPPLIERS		**PRINCIPAL BUYERS**	
West Germany	9,440	West Germany	9,580
U.S.A.	5,372	Belgium-Luxembourg	4,820
Belgium-Luxembourg	4,240	Italy	3,619
Italy	3,585	U.S.A.	2,935
Algeria	2,811	Switzerland	2,850
United Kingdom	2,580	Algeria	2,526
Netherlands	2,569	Netherlands	2,303

Germany (Federal Republic)

248,500 sq. km.; 60 M. inhab. (+ 1.3% per year); 240 inhab. per sq. km.

Capital: Bonn, 150,000 inhab.

Principal cities: West Berlin, 2.2 M.; Hamburg, 1.9 M.; Munich, 1.2 M.; Cologne, 850,000.

National currency: Deutsche mark = $.251.

Gross national product in 1965: 450 billion deutsch marks = $112.4 billion ($1,905 dollars per inhab.). Agriculture: 5%; all industries and construction: 53%; services: 42%.

Annual growth rate 1955–65: 5.6%.

Total budgetary expenditure in 1964: 90.49 billion deutsche marks.

Per capita consumption in 1964: Energy: 4,230 kg.; steel: 579 kg.

Major products (1965): Cereals: 15.3 M. tons; potatoes: 21.5 M. tons; cattle: 13.7 M. head; pigs: 17.7 M. head; milk: 21 M. tons; coal: 140 M. tons; lignite: 100 M. tons; lead ore: 50,000 tons; zinc ore: 110,000 tons; potassium: 2.5 M. tons; steel: 37 M. tons; cement: 34 M. tons; automobiles: 2.7 M. units; advanced industrial development, especially chemical industries.

Foreign trade 1965

IMPORTS CIF	M $U.S.	EXPORTS FOB	M $U.S.
Food, live animals, beverages, tobacco	3,650	Food, live animals, beverages, tobacco	412
Crude materials	2,824	Crude materials	518
Mineral fuels, lubricants, related materials	1,364	Mineral fuels, lubricants, related materials	728
Chemicals	840	Chemicals	2,077
Manufactured goods	4,084	Manufactured goods	3,987
Machinery, transportation materials	2,302	Machinery, transportation materials	8,270
Miscellaneous manufactured goods	1,127	Miscellaneous manufactured goods	1,572
Total	17,472	Total	17,892
PRINCIPAL SUPPLIERS		**PRINCIPAL BUYERS**	
U.S.A.	2,296	France	1,949
France	1,960	Netherlands	1,843
Netherlands	1,706	U.S.A.	1,436
Italy	1,641	Belgium-Luxembourg	1,391
Belgium-Luxembourg	1,353	Switzerland	1,158

Japan

370,000 sq. km.; 99 M. inhab. (+ 1% per year); 270 inhab. per sq. km.

Capital: Tokyo, 10.5 M. inhab.

Principal cities: Osaka, 3.25 M.; Nagoya, 1.9 M.; Yokohama, 1.65 M.; Kyoto, 1.35 M.; Kōbe, 1.2 M.; Kitakyushu, 1.1 M.

National currency: Yen = $.0028.

Gross national product in 1965: 30,100 billion yen = $83.6 billion ($853 per inhab.). Agriculture: 12%; all industries and construction: 38%; services: 50%.

Annual growth rate 1955–65: 9.6%.

Total budgetary expenditure in 1965: 3,990 billion yen.

Per capita consumption in 1964: Energy: 1,660 kg.; steel: 324 kg.

Major products (1965): Rice (paddy): 17 M. tons; tea: 83,000 tons; raw wood: 60 M. cubic meters; fish caught: 6.6 M. tons; coal: 50 M. tons; considerable production of copper, lead, manganese, mercury, molybdenum, silver, tungsten, and zinc ores; sulphur: 4 M. tons; naval construction: one-third of world production; steel: 27.5 M. tons; cement: 32.2 M. tons; all industries.

Foreign trade 1965

IMPORTS CIF	M$U.S.	EXPORTS FOB	M$U.S.
Food, live animals, beverages, tobacco	1,470	Food, beverages, tobacco	344
Crude materials	3,168	Crude materials	223
Mineral fuels, lubricants, related materials	1,626	Mineral fuels, lubricants, related materials	30
Chemicals	408	Chemicals	547
Manufactured goods	551	Manufactured goods	3,422
Machinery, transportation materials	711	Machinery, transportation materials	2,643
Miscellaneous manufactured goods	165	Miscellaneous manufactured goods	1,167
Total	8,170	Total	8,452
PRINCIPAL SUPPLIERS		PRINCIPAL BUYERS	
U.S.A.	2,366	U.S.A.	2,510
Australia	552	Liberia (ships)	371
Canada	357	Australia	313
Kuwait	305	Hong Kong	288
Philippines	254	China	245
Iran	247	Philippines	240

United Kingdom

244,000 sq. km.; 55 M. inhab. (+ 0.7% per year); 225 inhab. per sq. km.

Capital: London, 8,200,000 inhab.

Principal cities: Birmingham, 3.4 M.; Manchester: 2.5 M.; Leeds, 1.75 M.; Liverpool, 1.4 M.; Glasgow, 1.05 M.; Newcastle, 0.9 M.

National currency: £ Sterling = $2.81 (devaluation of 14.3% in November 1967).

Gross national product in 1965: £35.3 billion = $99 billion ($1,813 per inhab.). Agriculture: 4.5%; all industries and construction: 49.5%; services: 46%.

Annual growth rate 1955–65: 3.1%.

Total budgetary expenditure in 1964: £9.35 billion.

Per capita consumption in 1964: Energy: 5,079 kg.; steel: 438 kg.

Major products (1965): Cereals: 12 M. tons; cattle: 30 M. head; wool: 58,000 tons; coal: 190 M. tons; steel: 17.8 M. tons; cement: 17 M. tons; automobiles: 1.7 M. units; all industries, particularly chemical industries and naval construction.

Foreign trade 1965

IMPORTS CIF	M £	EXPORTS FOB	M £
Food, live animals, beverages tobacco	1,711	Food, live animals, beverages tobacco	298
Crude materials	1,046	Crude materials	144
Mineral fuels, lubricants, related mats.	617	Mineral fuels, lubricants, related mats.	133
Chemicals	283	Chemicals	439
Manuf. goods	1,088	Manuf. goods.	1,211
Machinery, transp. mats.	606	Machinery, transp. mats.	1,986
Misc. manuf. goods	275	Misc. manuf. goods	357
Total	5,763	Total	4,724
PRINCIPAL SUPPLIERS		**PRINCIPAL BUYERS**	
U.S.A.	674	U.S.A.	498
Canada	459	Australia	280
Netherlands	271	South Africa	264
West Germany	265	West Germany	255
Australia	220	Sweden	220
Sweden	215	Canada	200

United States

9,400,000 sq. km.; 197 M. inhab. (+ 1.6% per year); 21 inhab. per sq. km.

Capital: Washington, D.C., 2.3 M. inhab.

Principal cities: New York, 11.4 M.; Los Angeles, 6.6 M.; Chicago, 6.1 M.; Philadelphia, 4.6 M.; Detroit, 3.6 M.; San Francisco, 2.9 M.; Boston, 2.5 M.

National currency: Dollar = 4.90 francs = 0.357 pounds sterling.

Gross national product in 1965: $692 billion ($3,550 dollars per inhab.). Agriculture: 3.5%; all industries and construction: 38.5%; services: 58%.

Annual growth rate 1955–65: 3.4%.

Total budgetary expenditure in 1965: $122.4 billion.

Per capita consumption in 1964: Energy: 8,772 kg.; steel: 615 kg.

Major products (1965): Cereals: 165 M. tons; cotton: 3.3 M. tons; tobacco: 1.05 M. tons; cattle: 107 M. head; milk: 57 M. tons; coal: 475 M. tons; crude oil: 385 M. tons; natural gas: 444,000 M. cubic meters; iron ore: 48 M. tons; copper ore: 1.15 M. tons; lead ore: 260,000 tons; molybdenum ore: 30,000 tons (80% of world production); tungsten ore: 5,000 tons; bauxite: 2 M. tons; phosphates: 23 M. tons; steel: 122 M. tons; cement: 62 M. tons; automobiles: 9.3 M. units; all industries very highly developed.

Foreign trade 1965

IMPORTS FOB	M $U.S.	EXPORTS FOB	M$U.S.
Food, live animals, beverages, tobacco	3,579	Food, live animals, beverages, tobacco	4,516
Crude materials	3,036	Crude materials	2,856
Mineral fuels, lubricants, related materials	2,222	Mineral fuels, lubricants, related materials	946
Chemicals	781	Chemicals	2,402
Manufactured goods	5,556	Manufactured goods	3,258
Machinery, transportation materials	2,940	Machinery, transportation materials	10,016
Miscellaneous manufactured goods	1,973	Miscellaneous manufactured goods	1,612
Total	21,366	Total	27,003
PRINCIPAL SUPPLIERS		PRINCIPAL BUYERS	
Canada	4,832	Canada	5,643
Japan	2,414	Japan	2,080
United Kingdom	1,405	West Germany	1,650
West Germany	1,342	United Kingdom	1,615
Venezuela	1,021	Mexico	1,106
Mexico	638	Netherlands	1,088

Algeria

2,382,000 sq. km.; 11.3 M. inhab. (+2.6% per year); 4.7 inhab. per sq. km.

Capital: Algiers, 900,000 inhab.

Principal cities: Oran, 350,000; Constantine, 225,000; Annaba, 180,000.

National currency: Dinar = $.20.

Gross domestic product in 1965: Approximately 13,400 M. dinars ($230 per inhab. approx.). Agriculture: 20 to 22%; all industries: 25 to 27%.

Per capita consumption in 1964: Energy: 275 kg.; steel: 23 kg.

Major products: Wine: approximately 12 M. hectoliters; citrus: 450,000 tons; crude oil: 26.5 M. tons; natural gas: 2,000 M. cubic meters (major reserves); iron ore: 1.6 M. tons; zinc and lead ore; phosphates: 350,000 tons (1963), 73,000 tons (1964); cement: 730,000 tons; a steelworks is being constructed at Annaba, alfalfa, market-gardening.

Foreign trade 1963 *

IMPORTS CIF	M Dinars	EXPORTS FOB	M Dinars
		Crude petroleum	2,131
		Wine	465
		Citrus	168
		Iron ore	148
(Lack of significant figures)		Fresh vegetables	53
		Phosphates	34
		Vegetable preps.	28
		Raw hides and skins	25
		Dates	24
Total	3,090	Total	3,476
PRINCIPAL SUPPLIERS 1962		**PRINCIPAL BUYERS 1962**	
France	1,372	France	806
U.S.A.	107	United Kingdom	39
Morocco	46	Italy	24
Ivory Coast	39		
Italy	34		

* Provisional figures = c.92% of the total.

Angola

1,247,000 sq. km.; 5,200,000 inhab. (+ 1.4% per year); 4.2 inhab. per sq. km. (of which 110,000 are Europeans).

Capital: Luanda, 250,000 inhab.

Currency: Escudo: $.034.

Gross domestic product in 1965: Approximately 11.3 billion escudos ($80 per inhab. approx.).

Per capita consumption in 1964: Energy: 98 kg.

Major products: Coffee: 185,000 tons; sisal, cotton, tobacco, cocoa, sugar, palm nuts, wax; cattle: 1,300,000 head; crude oil: 900,000 tons; diamonds: 4% of world production; resources in iron, copper, and manganese; fish caught: approximately 300,000 tons.

Foreign trade 1965

IMPORTS CIF	M Escudos	EXPORTS FOB	M Escudos
Iron and steel products	562	Coffee beans	2,687
Automobiles and parts	541	Diamonds	904
Wines	430	Maize	283
Cotton piece-goods	377	Sisal	275
Medicines	150	Fish meal	175
Tractors	149	Iron ore	145
		Sugar	113
Total	5,601	Total	5,745
PRINCIPAL SUPPLIERS		**PRINCIPAL BUYERS**	
Portugal	2,661	Portugal	2,033
United Kingdom	627	U.S.A.	1,324
West Germany	459	Netherlands	679
U.S.A.	441	West Germany	312
		France	247

Cameroons

475,400 sq. km.; 5,250,000 inhab. (+ 2.2% per year); 11 inhab. per sq. km.

Capital: Yaoundé, 125,000 inhab.

Principal port: Douala, 200,000 inhab.

National currency: Franc CFA.

Gross domestic product in 1963: 149 billion francs CFA ($117 per inhab.).

Annual growth rate 1960–65: Approximately 7%.

Per capita consumption in 1964: Energy: 71 kg.

Major products: Coffee: 50,000–60,000 tons; bananas: 180,000 tons; cocoa: 95,000 tons; groundnuts: 170,000 tons; cotton seed: 60,000 tons; wood: nearly 6 M. cubic meters; cattle: 1,750,000 head; rubber: 12,000 tons; manioc, millet and sorghum, palm nuts; production of aluminum (53,000 tons) based on aluminum oxide imported from Guinea. Aluminum rolling mill under construction.

Foreign trade 1964

IMPORTS CIF	M Francs CFA	EXPORTS FOB	M Francs CFA
Food, live animals, beverages, tobacco	5,758	Food, live animals, tobacco (of which coffee, cocoa)	20,193 (17,758)
Crude materials	580	Crude materials (principally wood, cotton)	7,583
Mineral fuels, lubricants, related materials	2,128	Aluminum and alloys	5,115
Chemicals	4,679		
Manufactured goods	10,117		
Machinery, transp. mats.	7,173		
Misc. manufactured goods	3,219		
Total	32,836	Total	34,516
PRINCIPAL SUPPLIERS		**PRINCIPAL BUYERS**	
France	17,310	France	18,573
West Germany	2,089	Netherlands	4,612
United Kingdom	1,826	U.S.A.	2,365
U.S.A.	1,552	West Germany	2,109
Guinea	1,545	United Kingdom	2,006
Japan	1,502	Italy	1,416

Congo-Kinshasa

2,345,000 sq. km.; 15,650,000 inhab. (+ 2.1% per year); 6.7 inhab. per sq. km.

Capital: Kinshasa, 410,000 inhab.

Principal cities: Elisabethville, 185,000 inhab.; Stanleyville: 130,-000; Luluabourg, 120,000; Jadotville, 80,000.

National currency in 1965: Franc = $.0056; 1967: zaire = $2.

Gross domestic product in 1965: 211 billion francs ($75 per inhab.). Agriculture: approximately 27%; mines: approximately 20%; industrial manufactures: approximately 11%.

Per capita consumption in 1964: Energy: 79 kg.; steel: 5 kg.

Major products: Copper ore: 290,000 tons (sixth in the world); diamonds: 50% of world production; gold: 7,000 kg.; manganese ore: 170,000 tons (eighth in the world); cobalt; zinc ore: 120,000 tons; tin concentrate: approximately 6,500 tons; cement: 230,000 tons; palm oil: 215,000 tons; palm nuts: 125,000 tons; coffee: 60,000 tons; rubber: 35,000 tons; groundnuts: 120,000 tons; cocoa, cotton, manioc.

Foreign trade 1963, 1964, 1965

IMPORTS CIF 1963	M Francs	EXPORTS FOB 1965	M Francs
Food, live animals,		Copper	28,862
beverages, tobacco	5,439	Palm oil	3,587
Crude materials	362	Diamonds	3,498
Mineral fuels, lubricants,		Zinc ore, alloys, concentrates	3,217
related materials	1,962	Tin ore, alloys, concentratres	2,739
Chemicals	1,518	Cobalt	2,731
Manufactured goods	4,248	Coffee	2,572
Machinery, transp. materials	5,192		
Misc. manufactured goods	878		
Total	19,755	Total	49,310
PRINCIPAL SUPPLIERS 1964		**PRINCIPAL BUYERS 1964**	
Belgium-Luxembourg	15,454	Belgium-Luxembourg	11,938
U.S.A.	10,301	United Kingdom	3,833
West Germany	2,885	Italy	3,760
		France	2,984
		West Germany	1,525

Ethiopia

1,222,000 sq. km.; 22,650,000 inhab. (+ 1.7% per year); 18.5
  inhab. per sq. km.

Capital: Addis Ababa, 520,000 inhab.

Principal cities: Asmara: 140,000 inhab.; Harar, 50,000.

National currency: Ethiopian dollar = $.40 U.S.

Gross domestic product in 1965: 3,400 M. $Eth. ($60 U.S. per
  inhab. approx.). Agriculture: 65%; all industries: 7%. The
  economy is one of the most backward in the world.

Major products: Coffee: 135,000 tons; cereals (maize, barley);
  cotton; oil seeds; vegetables (poor productivity); cattle: 25
  M. head; sheep: 25 M. head.

Foreign trade 1965

IMPORTS CIF	M $ Ethiop.	EXPORTS FOB	M $ Ethiop.
Food, live animals, beverages, tobacco	25	Coffee	188
Crude materials	18	Raw hides and skins	24
Mineral fuels, lubricants, related materials	24	Oilseeds, etc.	23
Chemicals	27	Vegetables	15
Manufactured goods	95	Meat and preparations	7
Machinery, transp. materials	141		
Misc. manufactured goods	43		
Total	376	Total	283
PRINCIPAL SUPPLIERS		**PRINCIPAL BUYERS**	
Italy	67	U.S.A.	157
Japan	57	Italy	19
U.S.A.	44	Saudi Arabia	13
West Germany	40	West Germany	11
United Kingdom	34		
France	18		

Ghana

238,500 sq. km.; 7,900,000 inhab. (+ 2.4% per year); 33 inhab. per sq. km.

Capital: Accra, 400,000 inhab.

Principal cities: Kumasi, 200,000; Takoradi (port), 110,000.

National currency in 1965: Ghanaian pound = 1 pound sterling = $2.80. (In July 1965, devaluation of about 30%.) 1 cedi = 0.417 pounds.

Gross domestic product in 1964: 685 M. Ghanaian pounds ($250 per inhab.).

Average annual growth rate 1958–65: 3.6%.

Per capita consumption in 1964: Energy: 120 kg.; steel: 11 kg.

Total budgetary expenditure in 1965: 200 M. pounds.

Major products: Cocoa: 450,000 tons (first in the world); manganese ore: 250,000 tons (sixth in the world); gold: 25,000 kg. (sixth in the world); wood; diamonds: approximately 10% of world production; bauxite: 250,000 tons.

Foreign trade 1965

IMPORTS CIF	M Cedis	EXPORTS FOB	M Cedis
Food, amimals, tobacco	45	Cocoa (beans, butter)	179
Petroleum and products	16	Logs and lumber	30
Chemicals	24	Industrial diamonds	16
Industrial goods	130	Manganese ores and concs.	11
Machinery, transp. equip.	125		
Misc. manuf. goods	28		
Total	382	Total	249
PRINCIPAL SUPPLIERS		**PRINCIPAL BUYERS**	
United Kingdom	99	U.S.A.	42
West Germany	35	United Kingdom	32
U.S.A.	33	Netherlands	28
U.S.S.R.	26	West Germany	27
Netherlands	19	U.S.S.R.	26
Poland	17	Italy	11
Japan	17		

Guinea

246,000 sq. km.; 3,600,000 inhab. (+ 2.7% per year); 14.3 inhab. per sq. km.

Capital: Conakry: 125,000 inhab.

Principal cities: Kankan, 35,000 inhab.; Boké, 15,000, growing rapidly.

National currency: Franc CFA = $.004.

Gross domestic product in 1965: 96 billion francs ($110 per inhab. approx.).

Per capita consumption in 1964: Energy: 101 kg.

Major products: Bauxite; 1.8 M. tons (sixth in the world); aluminum oxide: 500,000 tons; iron ore, gold, diamonds, bananas, coffee, groundnuts, palm nuts, pineapples. The production of aluminum oxide is expected to expand and the production of aluminum to be undertaken.

Foreign trade 1962*

IMPORTS CIF	M Francs	EXPORTS FOB	M Francs
Rice	1,546	Aluminum oxide	6,631
Other foods, tobacco	c. 1,500	Bananas	1,120
Petroleum products	1,188	Oil seeds	1,050
Chemicals	1,052	Coffee	712
Machinery, transp. equip.	c. 3,000	Iron ore	612
Manufactured goods	c. 8,800	Diamonds	498
Total	16,195	Total	11,086
PRINCIPAL SUPPLIERS		PRINCIPAL BUYERS	
U.S.S.R.	3,269	France	2,036
France	2,385	Cameroons	1,410
U.S.A.	1,814	U.S.A.	1,227
West Germany	1,252	Norway	1,173
Czechoslovakia	841	East Germany	725
Netherlands	650	Poland	690
		U.S.S.R.	625

*Last year with complete figures.

Ivory Coast

322,500 sq. km.; 3,850,000 inhab. (+3.1% per year); 11.7
  inhab. per sq. km.
Capital: Abidjan, 320,000 inhab.
Principal city: Bouaké, 80,000 inhab.
National currency: Franc CFA = $.004.
Gross domestic product in 1964: 235 billion francs CFA ($250
  per inhab. approx.).
Per capita consumption in 1964: Energy: 107 kg.
Major products: Coffee: 300,000 tons (third in the world); cocoa:
  130,000 tons (fourth in the world). Considerable quantities
  are produced of: bananas; pineapples; palm oil; wood: 7.5
  M. cubic meters; manganese ore: 61,000 tons; oil extraction,
  canneries, textile industry.

Foreign trade 1965

IMPORTS CIF	M Francs CFA	EXPORTS FOB	M Francs CFA
Food, animals, tobacco	8,281	Coffee	26,253
Petroleum and products	3,248	Raw or semi-proc. wood	18,156
Chemicals	3,773	Cocoa	12,069
Manufactured goods	23,247	Bananas	2,796
Machinery, transp. equip.	16,479	Prepared fruit	1,281
		Manganese ores and conc.	750
Total	58,301	Total	68,418
PRINCIPAL SUPPLIERS		PRINCIPAL BUYERS	
France	36,379	France	25,771
West Germany	3,428	U.S.A.	10,631
U.S.A.	3,161	Italy	6,005
Italy	1,882	Netherlands	4,739
		West Germany	4,534

Kenya

583,000 sq. km.; 9,500,000 inhab. (+2.9% per year); 16.4 inhab. per sq. km.

Capital: Nairobi, 330,000 inhab.

Principal city (port): Mombasa, 200,000 inhab.

National currency: East African shilling = $.14.

Gross domestic product in 1965: 5,800 M. shillings ($92 per inhab.). Agriculture: 38%; all industries: 13%.

Annual growth rate 1958–65: 3.2%

Per capita consumption in 1964: Energy: 129 kg.

Total budgetary expenditure in 1965: 1,176 M. shillings.

Major products: Coffee: 45,000 tons; tea: 20,000 tons; sugarcane, sisal, bananas, pyrethrum; cattle: 7.5 M. head; gold: 390 kg.; copper; tourism is a major industry (game reserves and national parks).

Foreign trade 1965

IMPORTS CIF	1000 £	EXPORTS FOB	1000 £
Food, animals, tobacco	10,405	Coffee	14,111
Coal, coke, petroleum		Vegetable fibers	7,742
and products	10,281	Tea	6,085
Chemicals	8,345	Petroleum products	4,670
Manuf. goods	23,474	Meat and preparations	2,468
Machinery, transp. equip.	22,959	Pyrethrum	2,230
Misc. manuf. goods	6,058	Raw hides and skins	1,742
Total	88,916	Total	51,870
PRINCIPAL SUPPLIERS		PRINCIPAL BUYERS	
United Kingdom	25,164	United Kingdom	10,138
Japan	9,058	West Germany	7,374
U.S.A.	8,511	U.S.A.	2,643
West Germany	6,147	Netherlands	2,038
Iran	4,149		

Madagascar (Malagasy Republic)

596,000 sq. km.; 6,600,000 inhab. (+ 3.3% per year); 11 inhab. per sq. km.

Capital: Tananarive, 300,000 inhab.

Principal cities: Tamatave, 55,000 inhab. (main port); Tuléar, 45,000; Majunga, 40,000; Fianarantsoa, 40,000.

National currency: Franc CFA = $.004.

Gross domestic product in 1965: 176 billion francs CFA ($110 per inhab.).

Per capita consumption in 1964: Energy: 37 kg.

Major products: Coffee: 65,000 tons; rice: 1,270,000 tons; cotton, sugarcane, vanilla, sisal; cattle (Zébus): 9 M. head; uranium, mica, graphite, gold, chrome.

Foreign trade 1965

IMPORTS CIF	M Francs CFA	EXPORTS FOB	M Francs CFA
Food, beverages, tobacco	6,481	Coffee	7,133
Petroleum and products	1,844	Spices	3,531
Chemicals	3,101	(of which: vanilla)	(2,437)
Manufactured goods	9,822	Meats	1,649
Machinery, transp. equip.	8,606	Sisal and agave	1,340
Misc. manufactured goods	3,523	Vegetables	1,031
		Crude tobacco	877
Total	34,073	Total	22,632
PRINCIPAL SUPPLIERS		**PRINCIPAL BUYERS**	
France	21,313	France	10,122
Thailand	1,922	U.S.A.	6,092
U.S.A.	1,507	Réunion	1,310
West Germany	1,405	West Germany	1,036
		United Kingdom	603

Morocco

465,000 sq. km.; 14 M. inhab. (+3.2% per year); 30 inhab. per sq. km.

Capital: Rabat, 230,000 inhab.

Principal cities: Casablanca: 1.2 M. inhab.; Marrakesh, 250,000; Fez, 230,000; Meknes, 180,000; Tangier, 150,000; Oujda, 130,000; Tetuán, 110,000.

National currency: Dirham = $.198.

National revenue in 1965: 11.5 billion DH.

Gross domestic product in 1965: 12 billion DH ($175 per inhab.). Agriculture: 32%; mines: 8% manufacturing industry: 14%.

Annual growth rate 1960–67: 3.2%

Per capita consumption in 1964: Energy: 149 kg.; steel: 16 kg.

Major products: Citrus: 575,000 tons; cattle: 13 M. head; tomatoes, cereals (barley, hard wheat, maize), grapes, almonds, olives, rice, cotton; natural phosphates: 10 M. tons (the world's main exporter); manganese ore: 150,000 to 200,000 tons; cobalt: 1,500 tons; lead ore: 75,000 tons; zinc ore: 45,000 tons; iron ore: approximately 600,000 tons; coal, antimony, copper; textile and food (sardine) industries; fisheries: 200,000 tons.

Foreign trade 1964

IMPORTS CIF	M Dirhams	EXPORTS FOB	M Dirhams
Food, live animals, beverages, tobacco	636	Phosphates	578
		Citrus	311
(of which sugar)	(327)	Fresh vegetables	269
Crude materials	213	Non-ferrous ores	164
Mineral fuels, lubricants,		Preserved fish	135
related materials	137	Wine	119
Chemicals	196	Cereals	65
Manufactured goods	570	Iron ore	40
Machinery, transp. materials	427	Preserved vegetables	32
Total	2,308	Total	2,186
PRINCIPAL SUPPLIERS		**PRINCIPAL BUYERS**	
France	879	France	958
U.S.A.	271	West Germany	182
Cuba (sugar)	186	Spain	132
West Germany	140	United Kingdom	108
		Belgium-Luxembourg	79

Mozambique

783,000 sq. km.: 7 M. inhab. (+ 1.3% per year); 9 inhab. per sq. km.

Capital: Lourenço Marques, 200,000 inhab.

Principal city: Beira, 50,000 inhab.

Currency: Escudo = $.034.

Gross domestic product in 1965: 12 billion escudos ($60 per inhab. approx.).

Per capita consumption in 1964: Energy: 132 kg.

Major products: Cotton: 35,000 tons; rice: 150,000 tons; tea: 10,000 tons; sisal, copra, sugarcane, maize, manioc, beans, timber; cattle: 1,150,000 head; coal: 280,000 tons; little developed resources in iron ore, bauxite, copper, gold; industry limited to the transformation of agricultural products.

Foreign trade 1965

IMPORTS CIF	M Escudos	EXPORTS FOB	M Escudos
		Oil seeds	680
		Raw cotton	554
		Raw sugar	292
(lack of significant figures)		Tea	205
		Wood	194
		Sisal	175
		Vegetable oils	170
Total	4,981	Total	3,107
PRINCIPAL SUPPLIERS		**PRINCIPAL BUYERS**	
Portugal	1,720	Portugal	1,151
United Kingdom	525	India	451
South Africa	524	South Africa	360
West Germany	385	U.S.A.	147
Iraq	244	United Kingdom	142
U.S.A.	206		

Nigeria

924,000 sq. km.; 58,500,000 inhab. (+ 2.0% per year); 63 inhab. per sq. km.

Capital: Lagos, 680,000 inhab.

Principal cities: Ibadan, 640,000 inhab.; Zaria, 175,000; Kano, 135,000; Oyo, 120,000; Iwo, 110,000; Enugu, 90,000.

National currency: Pound = $2.80.

Gross domestic product in 1965: £1,320 M. approximately ($65 per inhab. approx.). Agriculture: approximately 60%; all industries: approximately 10%.

Annual growth rate 1958–65: approximately 5%.

Total budgetary expenditure in 1963: £163 M.

Per capita consumption in 1964: Energy: 38 kg.; steel: 6 kg.

Major products: Palm oil: 400,000 tons (first in the world); cocoa: 300,000 tons (second in the world); rubber: 70,000 tons; groundnuts: 1,300,000 tons (third in the world); cotton; timber: 31 M. cubic meters; livestock; coal: 700,000 tons; tin concentrate: 9,000 tons (sixth in the world); crude oil: 6 M. tons.

Foreign trade 1965

IMPORTS CIF	M £	EXPORTS FOB	M £
Food, beverages, tobacco	25	Oil seeds	69
Crude materials	6	Crude or partly refined	
Petroleum products	17	petroleum	68
Chemicals	20	Cocoa	43
Manuf. goods	90	Vegetable oil	24
Machinery, transp. equip.	92	Rubber	11
Misc. manuf. goods	21	Cotton	6
		Wood	6
		Raw hides and skins	5
Total	275	Total	263
PRINCIPAL SUPPLIERS		**PRINCIPAL BUYERS**	
United Kingdom	85	United Kingdom	101
U.S.A.	33	Netherlands	32
West Germany	30	West Germany	28
Japan	26	U.S.A.	26
Italy	13	France	18
France	12		

Republic of South Africa

1,221,000 sq. km.; 18.3 M. inhab. (+ 2.4% per year); 15 inhab. per sq. km. (19% white, 68% black, 13% Indian and mixed blood.)

Capital: Pretoria, 440,000 inhab. Administrative capital: Capetown, 830,000 inhab.

Principal cities: Johannesburg, 1.2 M.; Durban, 700,000.

National currency: Rand = $1.395.

National income in 1964: 6,250 M. rand.

Gross domestic product in 1964: 7,590 M. rand ($625 per inhab. approx.). Agriculture: 9%; all industries (including construction): 40%.

Annual growth rate 1958–64: 5.6%.

Total budgetary expenditure in 1965: 1,547 M. rand.

Per capita consumption in 1964: Energy: 2,576 kg.; steel: 173 kg.

Major products: Gold: 950 tons (half the total world production); diamonds: about one-sixth of world production excluding the U.S.S.R.; uranium oxide: 3,800 tons; steel: 3.25 M. tons; coal: 50 M. tons; manganese ore: 600,000 tons; chrome ore: 400,000 tons; antimony ore: 13,000 tons; asbestos: 200,000 tons; sheep: 35 M. head; cattle: 13 M. head.

Foreign trade 1965

IMPORTS CIF	M Rands	EXPORTS FOB	M Rands
Food, animals, beverages, tobacco	78	Food, animals, beverages, tobacco	234
Crude materials	132	Crude materials	317
Coke, coal, petroleum prods.	93	Coke, coal, petroleum prods.	25
Chemicals	124	Chemicals	34
Manufactured goods	426	Manufactured goods	275
Machinery, transp. equip.	738	Machinery, transp. equip.	34
Misc. manufactured goods	122	Misc. manufactured goods	12
		Gold	766
Total	1,754	Total	1,817
PRINCIPAL SUPPLIERS		PRINCIPAL BUYERS	
United Kingdom	494	United Kingdom	356
U.S.A.	331	U.S.A.	100
West Germany	191	Japan	72
Japan	101	West Germany	55
Italy	70	Belgium-Luxembourg	45

Senegal

196,000 sq. km.; 3,550,000 inhab. (+ 2.3% per year); 17.8
   inhab. per sq. km.
Capital: Dakar, 400,000 inhab. (important port).
Principal cities: Kaolack, 90,000 inhab.; Thiès, 75,000; Saint-
   Louis, 70,000; Rufisque, 55,000.
National currency: Franc CFA = $.004.
Gross domestic product in 1965: 167 billion francs CFA ($194
   per inhab.).
Annual growth rate 1958–65: 0%.
Per capita consumption in 1964: Energy: 136 kg.
Major products: groundnuts: 1 M. tons (fourth in the world);
   rice: 100,000 tons; cotton, millet, garden vegetables; cattle:
   2 M. head; fisheries: 130,000 tons (especially tuna); phos-
   phates: 800,000 tons; salt, deposits of aluminum oxide,
   bauxite, iron; oil extraction, breweries, light textile industry.

Foreign trade 1965

IMPORTS CIF	M Francs CFA	EXPORTS FOB	M Francs CFA
Food, beverages, tobacco	14,801	Groundnut oil	13,143
Petroleum products	c. 2,000	Oil seeds	9,328
Crude materials	1,444	Phosphates	2,669
Chemicals	2,498	Oilseed cakes	2,553
Manufactured goods	10,847		
Machinery, transp. equip.	5,769		
Misc. manufactured goods	2,352		
Total	40,554	Total	31,712
PRINCIPAL SUPPLIERS		**PRINCIPAL BUYERS**	
France	21,548	France	25,589
Cambodia	2,307	West Germany	869
West Germany	1,805	Madagascar	592
U.S.A.	1,665	Japan	588
Thailand	1,626	Italy	466
		United Kingdom	447

Southern Rhodesia

390,000 sq. km.; 4.4 M. inhab. (230,000 Europeans) (+ 3.2%
per year); 11 inhab. per sq. km.

Capital: Salisbury, 320,000 inhab.

Principal city: Bulawayo, 220,000 inhab.

Currency: Pound = $2.80.

National revenue in 1965: £338 M.

Gross domestic product in 1965: £380 M. ($250 per inhab.).
Agriculture: 19%; mines: 10%; industrial manufactures:
19%.

Annual growth rate 1958–65: 3.3%.

Total budgetary expenditure in 1966: £86 M.

Per capita consumption in 1964: Energy: 577 kg.; steel: 22 kg.

Major products: Maize: 500,000 tons; wheat, cotton; tobacco:
130,000 tons (fifth or sixth in the world); sugar: 170,000
tons; groundnuts, citrus, timber; cattle: 3.9 M. head; coal:
3 M. tons; iron ore; 500,000 tons; chrome: 200,000 tons
(second in the world); copper, antimony; gold: 18 tons;
tin, manganesite; asbestos: 140,000 tons (third in the world).

Foreign trade 1965

IMPORTS FOB	M £	EXPORTS FOB	M £
Food, beverages, tobacco	13	Raw tobacco	47
Crude materials	5	Asbestos	11
Petroleum products	6	Textiles and clothing	9
Chemicals	13	Sugar	7
Manuf. goods	31	Copper	7
Machinery, transp. equip.	38	Meat	6
Misc. manuf. goods	11	Iron and steel	6
		Chromium ore	4
Total	112	Total	142
PRINCIPAL SUPPLIERS		**PRINCIPAL BUYERS**	
United Kingdom	36	Zambia	36
South Africa	28	United Kingdom	31
U.S.A.	8	South Africa	15
Japan	7	West Germany	13
West Germany	5	Malawi	8
		Japan	7

Sudan

2,506,000 sq. km.; 13,900,000 inhab. (+ 2.8% per year); 5.5
inhab. per sq. km.; heterogeneous population.

Capital: Khartoum, 150,000 inhab. (conurbation: more than
300,000).

Principal cities: Port Sudan, 70,000 inhab.; Kassala, 50,000;
Atbara, 40,000.

National currency: Pound = $2.90.

Gross domestic product in 1964: £485 M. ($110 per inhab.).
Agriculture: 54%; all industries: 6%.

Average annual growth rate 1958–64: about 5%.

Per capita consumption in 1964: Energy: 60 kg.

Total budgetary expenditure in 1966: £100 M.

Principal products: Cotton: 175,000 tons (sixth or seventh in the
world); cattle: 7 M. head; sheep: 8 M. head; goats: 6 M.
head; salt: 60,000 tons. Secondary cereals, gum arabic, oil
seeds.

Foreign trade 1965

IMPORTS CIF	1000 £	EXPORTS FOB	1000 £
Food, beverages, tobacco	17,278	Raw cotton	31,195
Crude materials	1,380	Oilseeds	15,555
Coal, coke, petrol. prods.	3,479	Gum arabic	7,528
Chemicals	7,016	Oilseed cakes	3,786
Manuf. goods	22,461		
Machinery, transp. equip.	15,200		
Misc. manuf. goods	4,314		
Total	72,289	Total	67,139
PRINCIPAL SUPPLIERS		**PRINCIPAL BUYERS**	
United Kingdom	16,918	West Germany	7,182
Japan	6,819	Italy	7,144
India	6,490	United Kingdom	6,560
U.S.A.	4,728	China	5,365
West Germany	3,835	Netherlands	4,473
U.S.S.R.	2,583	U.S.S.R.	4,378

Tanzania

940,000 sq. km.; 10,300,000 inhab. (+ 1.4% per year); 11 inhab. per sq. km.

Capital: Dar-Es-Salaam, 135,000 inhab.

Principal city: Zanzibar, 65,000 inhab.

National currency: East African shilling = $.14.

National revenue in 1964: approximately 4,700 M. shillings.

Gross domestic product in 1964: approximately 5,200 M. shillings ($70 per inhab.). Agriculture: 55%; all industries: 7%.

Annual growth rate 1958–65: 3.1%

Total budgetary expenditure in 1966: 1,350 M. shillings.

Per capita consumption in 1964: Energy: 51 kg.

Major products: Sisal: 250,000 tons (first in the world); cloves: the greater part of world production; coffee: 35,000 tons; cotton: 50,000 tons; cattle: 8.3 M. head; tea, tobacco, rice, groundnuts; gold: 3,000 kg.; tin concentrate: 300 tons; diamonds: 2.5% of world production.

Foreign trade 1965

IMPORTS CIF	M £	EXPORTS FOB	M £
Food, beverages, tobacco	4	Sisal and agave fiber	14
Crude materials	1	Raw cotton	12
Petroleum products	2	Coffee	9
Chemicals	4	Diamonds	7
Manuf. goods	20	Cashew nuts	4
Machinery, transp. equip.	17	Cloves	2
Misc. manuf. goods	5		
Total	54	Total	67
PRINCIPAL SUPPLIERS		**PRINCIPAL BUYERS**	
United Kingdom	17	United Kingdom	19
Japan	5	India	6
West Germany	4	Hong Kong	5
Italy	4	West Germany	5
India	4	China	4
U.S.A.	3	U.S.A.	4

Tunisia

164,000 sq. km.; 4,800,000 inhab. (+ 2.1% per year); 29 inhab. per sq. km.

Capital: Tunis, 700,000 inhab. (conurbation).

Principal cities: Sfax, 75,000 inhab.; Sousse, 55,000; Bizerte, 50,000; Kairouan, 45,000.

National currency: Dinar = $1.905.

National revenue in 1965: 414 M. dinars.

Gross domestic product in 1965: 500 M. dinars ($185 per inhab.). Agriculture: 22%; all industries: 18%.

Annual growth rate 1958–65: 5.3%.

Per capita consumption in 1964: Energy: 244 kg.; steel: 21 kg.

Major products: Olive oil: 100,000 tons; wine: 1,800,000 hecto-liters; cereals, dates, garden vegetables, citrus, cork, esparto grass, fish; phosphates: 2,800,000 tons; iron ore: 600,000 tons; lead and zinc ores; salt; industry: oil extraction, canneries; cement: 450,000 tons; the development of oil deposits is planned.

Foreign trade 1965

IMPORTS CIF	M Dinars	EXPORTS FOB	M Dinars
Food, live animals, beverages, tobacco	18	Olive oil	14
Crude materials	7	Natural phosphates	13
Mineral fuels, lubricants, related mat.	7	Phosphate fertilizers	9
Chemicals	8	Citrus	3
Manuf. goods	39	Wine	3
Machinery, transp. mats.	40	Iron ore	3
Misc. manuf. goods	6	Lead	2
Total	129	Total	63
PRINCIPAL SUPPLIERS		**PRINCIPAL BUYERS**	
France	50	France	20
U.S.A.	21	Italy	8
Italy	9	United Kingdom	3
West Germany	7	Yugoslavia	3
United Kingdom	5	Greece	2
U.S.S.R.	3	Algeria	2

Uganda

236,000 sq. km.; 7.7 M. inhab. (+2.5% per year); 32.6 inhab.
  per sq. km.
Capital: Kampala, 140,000 inhab. (conurbation).
Principal city: Jinja, 35,000 inhab.
National currency: East African shilling = $.14.
Gross domestic product in 1965: 224 M. EA pounds ($83 per
  inhab.). Agriculture: 59%; all industries: 12%.
Annual growth rate 1958–65: 3.8%.
Total budgetary expenditure in 1966: 1,200 M. shillings.
Per capita consumption in 1964: Energy: 36 kg.
Major products: Coffee: 180,000 tons; cotton: 80,000 tons;
  groundnuts: 160,000 tons; tea: 7,000 tons; cattle: 3.5 M.
  head; timber: 11 M. cubic meters; copper ore: 20,000
  tons; cobalt ore and tin.

Foreign trade 1965

IMPORTS CIF	1000 £	EXPORTS FOB	1000 £
Food, beverages, tobacco	2,146	Coffee	30,421
Crude materials	612	Raw cotton	16,762
Petroleum products	446	Copper and alloys	7,994
Animal and vegetable oils		Tea	2,388
and fats	860		
Chemicals	3,100		
Manuf. goods	16,830		
Machinery, trans. equip.	14,847		
Total	40,854	Total	62,713
PRINCIPAL SUPPLIERS		**PRINCIPAL BUYERS**	
United Kingdom	15,679	U.S.A.	14,092
Japan	4,157	United Kingdom	10,697
West Germany	3,812	Belgium-Luxembourg	7,017
India	1,946	China	6,237
U.S.A.	1,937	India	3,477
Italy	1,636	Canada	2,165
France	1,575		

United Arab Republic

1 M. sq. km.; 30 M. inhab. (+ 2.9% per year); 30 inhab. per sq. km.

Capital: Cairo, 3,500,000 inhab.

Principal cities: Alexandria, 1,600,000 inhab.; Port Saïd, 270,000; Suez, 210,000; Tanta, 190,000; Mansura, 160,000; Ismailia, 120,000.

National currency: Egyptian pound = $2.30.

Gross domestic product in 1964: 2,050 M. Egyptian pounds ($155 per inhab.). Agriculture: approximately 23%; all industries: approximately 25%.

Annual growth rate 1958–65: 6.5%.

Total budgetary expenditure in 1965: 742 M. Egyptian pounds (1964: 480 M.).

Per capita consumption in 1964: Energy: 321 kg.; steel: 24 kg.

Major products: Cotton: 500,000 tons (fourth in the world); sugar: 400,000 tons; cotton seed: 900,000 tons (fifth in the world); maize: 1,900,000 tons; rice: 2 M. tons; wheat: 1,500,000 tons; crude oil: 6.5 M. tons; steel: 150,000 tons; textile, food, fertilizer industries; Suez Canal revenue: $200 M.

Foreign trade 1965

IMPORTS CIF	M £ Egypt.	EXPORTS FOB	M £ Egypt.
Food, animals, tobacco	106	Raw cotton	146
Crude materials	39	Textiles, fabrics	44
Coal, coke, petroleum		Rice	20
and products	33	Petroleum and products	17
Chemicals	51	Fish vegetables	10
Manufactured goods	72		
Machinery, transp. equip.	95		
Total	406	Total	261
PRINCIPAL SUPPLIERS		PRINCIPAL BUYERS	
U.S.A.	82	U.S.S.R.	57
West Germany	38	Czechoslovakia	27
U.S.S.R.	37	China	20
India	24	West Germany	15
Italy	24	Italy	12
France	21	India	11

Zambia

752,600 sq. km.; 3.8 M. inhab. (75,000 Europeans) (+ 2.9% per year); 5 inhab. per sq. km.

Capital: Lusaka, 100,000 inhab.

Principal cities: Ndola, 95,000 inhab.; Livingstone, 35,000.

National currency: Pound = $2.80.

Gross domestic product in 1965: £320 M. ($220 per inhab. approx.). Agriculture: 10%; mines: 42%; manufacturing industry: 7%.

Annual growth rate 1958–65: 6.1%.

Total budgetary expenditure in 1964: £55 M.

Per capita consumption in 1964: Energy: 431 kg.; steel: 3 kg.

Major products: Coffee, tobacco; cattle: 1.3 M. head; copper ore: 630,000 tons (fourth in the world); manganese ore; cobalt ore: 1,400 tons (fifth in the world); lead and zinc ore, etc.; problem of outlet to the sea: at first through Beira (Mozambique), now through Tanzania.

Foreign trade 1965

IMPORTS FOB	M £	EXPORTS FOB	M £
Food, animals, beverages, tobacco	10	Crude and semi-crude copper	172
Crude mats., coke, coal, and pet. prods.	7	Other non-ferrous metals	8
Electric energy	5	Raw tobacco	2
Chemicals	10		
Manuf. goods	25		
Machinery, transp. equip.	35		
Misc. manuf. goods	13		
Total	105	Total	188
PRINCIPAL SUPPLIERS		PRINCIPAL BUYERS	
Southern Rhodesia	36	United Kingdom	72
United Kingdom	21	West Germany	25
South Africa	21	Japan	23
U.S.A.	7	Italy	16
Japan	4	France	14
West Germany	3	South Africa	13

Argentina

2,777,000 sq. km.; 22.7 M. inhab. (+1.6% per year); 8.1 inhab. per sq. km.

Capital: Buenos Aires, 3 M. inhab. (conurbation: 7 M).

Principal cities: Rosario, 680,000; Córdoba, 650,000; La Plata, 400,000.

National currency in 1965: Peso = $.006 ($1.09 = approximately 170 pesos). *In 1967,* peso =$.00286 ($1.00 = 350 pesos).

Gross domestic product in 1965: Approximately 3,260 billion pesos ($845 per inhab.). Agriculture: 16%; all industries: 37%.

Annual growth rate 1958–65: 3.2%.

Total budgetary expenditure in 1965: 387 billion pesos.

Per capita consumption in 1964: Energy: 1,242 kg.; steel: 93 kg.

Major products: Wheat: 10 M. tons; maize: 5.2 M. tons; flax seed: 800,000 tons (first in the world); wine: 20 M. hectoliters; cattle: 43 M. head (fourth in the world); sheep: 45 M. head (fourth in the world); pigs: 3.5 M. head; wool: 190,000 tons; crude oil: 14 M. tons; natural gas: 3,700 M. cubic meters; steel: 1.3 M. tons; cement: 3 M. tons; food and textile industries.

Foreign trade 1965

IMPORTS CIF	M $U.S.	EXPORTS FOB	M $U.S.
Food, animals, beverages, tobacco	73	Cereals (wheat, maize)	582
Crude materials	183	Fresh or frozen meat	272
Coke, coal, petroleum products	115	Wool	117
Chemicals	130	Canned meat, etc.	53
Manufactured goods	347	Raw hides and skins	48
Machinery, transportation equipment	301	Linseed oil	47
Miscellaneous manufactured goods	40		
Total	1,199	Total	1,493
PRINCIPAL SUPPLIERS		**PRINCIPAL BUYERS**	
U.S.A.	273	Italy	239
Brazil	162	Netherlands	161
West Germany	110	United Kingdom	153
Italy	80	Brazil	107
United Kingdom	73	West Germany	99
France	46	U.S.A.	95
Japan	44	U.S.S.R.	87

Brazil

8,512,000 sq. km.; 85 M. inhab. (+ 3% per year); 10 inhab. per sq. km.

Capital: Brasilia, 250,000 inhab.

Principal cities: Río de Janeiro, 3.7 M. inhab.; São Paulo, 3.5 M.; Recife, 900,000; Belo Horizonte, 800,000.

National currency: Cruzeiro = $.0005 (1965 rate). Since 1958: 1 heavy cruzeiro = $31.25.

Gross domestic product in 1965: Approximately 31,000 billion cruzeiros ($210 per inhab.). Agriculture: 29%; all industries: 28%.

Annual growth rate 1958–65: 4.5%.

Total budgetary expenditure in 1965 (Federal government and states): 5,270 billion cruzeiros.

Per capita consumption in 1964: Energy: 364 kg.; steel: 43 kg.

Major products: Coffee: 1.6 M. tons (first in the world); rice: 6 M. tons; cotton: 600,000 tons; groundnuts: 600,000 tons; cocoa: 150,000 tons; maize: 10 M. tons; sugar: 3.4 M. tons; cattle: 80 M. head; pigs: 55 M. head; sheep: 21 M. head; timber; iron ore: 10 M. tons; manganese ore: 600,000 tons; steel: M. tons; textile industries (cotton) and others.

trade 1965

IMPORTS CIF	M $U.S.	EXPORTS FOB	M $U.S.
imals	203	Coffee	707
terials	43	Iron ore and concentrates	103
e, petroleum and		Raw cotton	96
s	225	Wood	63
	174	Raw sugar	57
red goods	156	Iron and steel	44
transportation		Cocoa	41
t	244	Vegetable oils	35
us manufactured		Non-ferrous minerals	34
	33		
otal	1,096	Total	1,595
AL SUPPLIERS		PRINCIPAL BUYERS	
	325	U.S.A.	520
	132	West Germany	141
	96	Argentina	141
	82	Italy	85
y	37	Netherlands	81
	35	United Kingdom	62
	33	France	56

Bolivia

1,098,500 sq. km.; 3,750,000 inhab. (+ 1.4% per yea
   inhab. per sq. km.

Capital: Sucre, 70,000 inhab.

Principal city: La Paz, 370,000 inhab.

National currency: Peso = $.084.

Gross domestic product in 1965: 7,230 M. pesos
   inhab.). Agriculture: 23%; mines: 16%; indu

Annual growth rate 1958–65: 4.5% approximately

Total budgetary expenditure in 1964: 2,460 M. pe

Per capita consumption in 1964: Energy: 173 kg.

Major products: Cattle: 2.8 M. head; sheep: 7.
   mony ore: 9,700 tons (third in the world)
   25,000 tons (second or third in the worl
   centrate: 1,400 tons; copper, lead, and sil

Foreign trade 1965

IMPORTS CIF	M $U.S.	EXP Interna
(Incomplete and insignificant figures)		Tin ore and Lead ore Silver Zinc ore
Wheat flour	11	Wolfram Other m
Total	126	
PRINCIPAL SUPPLIERS		PF
U.S.A.	59	Unit
Japan	17	U.S.
West Germany	15	Wes
Argentina	7	
United Kingdom	7	

Chile

742,000 sq. km.; 8,800,000 inhab. (+ 2.3% per year); 12 inhab. per sq. km.

Capital: Santiago, 2,400,000 inhab. (conurbation).

Principal cities: Valparaiso, 300,000 inhab.; Concepción, 180,000; Viña del Mar, 150,000; Temuco, 130,000.

National currency: Escudo = $.32.

Gross domestic product in 1965: 20,800 M. escudos ($650 per inhab.). Agriculture: 10% mines: 8%; industries: 18%.

Annual growth rate 1958–65: 4.1%.

Total budgetary expenditure in 1965: 3,860 M. escudos.

Per capita consumption in 1964: Energy: 1,078 kg.; steel: 74 kg.

Major products: Wine: 5 M. hectoliters; fish: 1 M. tons; sheep: 6.5 M. head; copper ore: 800,000 tons (second in the world); iron ore: 7 M. tons; molybdenum: 3,800 tons (third in the world); steel: 500,000 tons; cement: 1.2 M. tons.

Foreign trade 1963, 1964, 1965

IMPORTS CIF	M Pesos*	EXPORTS FOB	M Pesos*
Food, animals, beverages tobacco	617	Copper (ingots and bars)	1,847
Crude materials	277	Iron ore	338
Coke, coal, petroleum prods.	152	Various minerals and concentrates	222
Chemicals	384	Saltpeter	134
Manuf. goods	360	Copper wire	90
Machinery, transp. equip.	1,076	Fish meal	77
Misc. manuf. goods	166		
Total	3,094	Total	3,038
PRINCIPAL SUPPLIERS		**PRINCIPAL BUYERS**	
U.S.A.	1,151	U.S.A.	1,034
West Germany	309	West Germany	440
Argentina	248	United Kingdom	375
United Kingdom	186	Japan	360
Peru	116	Netherlands	351
Total	2,930	Total	3,339

* Unit of exchange = 6 ounces of gold

Colombia

1,138,000 sq. km.; 18.6 M. inhab. (+ 3.2% per year); 16.3 inhab. per sq. km.

Capital: Bogotá, 1,750,000 inhab.

Principal cities: Cali, 830,000 inhab.; Medellín, 800,000; Baranquilla, 540,000.

National currency: Peso = $.111 (official rate).

Gross domestic product in 1965: approximately 59 billion pesos ($280 per inhab.). Agriculture: 32%; all industries: 22%.

Annual growth rate 1958–65: 4.5%.

Total budgetary expenditure in 1965: 4,600 M. pesos.

Per capita consumption in 1964: Energy: 494 kg.; steel: 31 kg.

Major products: Coffee: 480,000 tons (second in the world); cattle: 16 M. head; maize: 1.1 M. tons; tobacco: 43,000 tons; bananas, cotton; sugar: 400,000 tons; crude oil: 8.5 M. tons; gold: 11,000 kg.; steel: 200,000 tons; cement: 2 M. tons.

Foreign trade 1965

IMPORTS CIF	M $U.S.	EXPORTS FOB	M $U.S.
Food, beverages, tobacco	26	Coffee	344
Crude materials	38	Crude oil	88
Chemicals	72	Bananas	19
Manufactured goods	70	Refined petroleum products	8
Machinery, transportation equipment	206	Raw cotton	8
Miscellaneous manufactured goods	12		
Total	454	Total	539
PRINCIPAL SUPPLIERS		PRINCIPAL BUYERS	
U.S.A.	212	U.S.A.	252
West Germany	52	West Germany	63
United Kingdom	23	Netherlands	29
Canada	19	Trinidad and Tobago	28
Japan	16	Spain	25
Sweden	13	United Kingdom	21

Dominican Republic

48,700 sq. km.; 3,730,000 inhab. (+ 3.5% per year); 76.5 inhab. per sq. km.

Capital: Santo Domingo, 400,000 inhab.

National currency: Peso = $1.00.

Gross domestic product in 1964: 1,085 M. pesos ($310 per inhab.). Agriculture: 24%; all industries: 18%.

Annual growth rate 1958–64: 5.2%.

Total budgetary expenditure in 1964: 196 M. pesos.

Per capita consumption in 1964: Energy: 209 kg.

Major products: Sugar: 850,000 tons; cocoa: 40,000 tons; coffee: 40,000 tons; groundnuts: 50,000 tons; maize: 100,000 tons; rice: 150,000 tons; tobacco: 30,000 tons; bananas: 20 M. tons; bauxite: 800,000 tons; cement: 300,000 tons; food canneries.

Foreign trade 1964

IMPORTS FOB	M Pesos	EXPORTS FOB	M Pesos
(Incomplete and insignificant figures)		Sugar	86
		Coffee	30
		Tobacco	15
		Cocoa	12
		Bauxite	9
		Bananas	5
Total	192	Total	178
PRINCIPAL SUPPLIERS		PRINCIPAL BUYERS	
U.S.A.	102	U.S.A.	118
West Germany	13	United Kingdom	11
Japan	12	Italy	9
United Kingdom	9	West Germany	5
Netherlands	8		
Canada	8		

Ecuador

283,500 sq. km.; 5,250,000 inhab. (+ 3.2% per year); 18.5
inhab. per sq. km.

Capital: Quito, 380,000 inhab.

Principal city: Guayaquil, 530,000 inhab.

National currency: Sucre = $.055.

Gross domestic product in 1965: 20.8 billion sucres ($220 per
inhab.). Agriculture: 34%; all industries: 21%.

Total budgetary expenditure in 1965: 3,450 M. sucres.

Annual growth rate 1958–65: 4.3%.

Per capita consumption in 1964: Energy: 195 kg.

Major products: Bananas: 2.2 M. tons; coffee: 50,000 tons; cocoa:
50,000 tons; rice: 180,000 tons; potatoes: 325,000 tons;
sugar: 160,000 tons; gold: 600 kg.; crude oil: 375,000 tons;
cement: 300,000 tons.

Foreign trade 1964

IMPORTS FOB	M $U.S.	EXPORTS FOB	M $U.S.
Food, beverages, tobacco	16	Bananas	84
Petroleum and products	8	Coffee	37
Chemicals	20	Sugar	7
Manufactured goods	40		
Machinery, transportation equipment	47		
Miscellaneous manufactured goods	7		
Total	148	Total	143
PRINCIPAL SUPPLIERS		PRINCIPAL BUYERS	
U.S.A.	69	U.S.A.	66
West Germany	17	West Germany	21
Belgium-Luxembourg	9	Japan	9
United Kingdom	8	Belgium-Luxembourg	6
Japan	6	Colombia	6
Canada	5	Netherlands	5

Guatemala

109,000 sq. km.; 4,600,000 inhab. (+ 3.2% per year); 42 inhab.
per sq. km.
Capital: Guatemala, 450,000 inhab.
Principal cities: Quezàltenango, 50,000 inhab.; Puerto Barrios,
30,000 inhab.
National currency: Quetzal = $1.00.
Gross domestic product in 1965: 1,430 M. quetzals ($322 per
inhab.). Agriculture: 28%: all industries: 16%.
Annual growth rate 1958–65: 5.8%.
Total budgetary expenditure in 1964: 107 M. quetzals.
Per capita consumption in 1964: Energy: 175 kg.
Major products: Bananas: 22 M. tons (United Fruit); coffee:
100,000 tons; maize: 575,000 tons; cotton: 70,000 tons;
cotton seed: 110,000 tons; sugar: 150,000 tons; cement:
180,000 tons.

Foreign trade 1965

IMPORTS CIF	M Quetzales	EXPORTS FOB	M Quetzales
Food, beverages, tobacco	23	Coffee	92
Petroleum and products	16	Raw cotton	34
Chemicals	39	Meat	5
Manufactured goods	61	Sugar	5
Machinery, transp. equip.	66	Textiles	5
Misc. manufactured goods	19	Bananas	4
Total	229	Total	187
PRINCIPAL SUPPLIERS		**PRINCIPAL BUYERS**	
U.S.A.	97	U.S.A.	68
El Salvador	22	West Germany	25
West Germany	22	Japan	21
Japan	15	El Salvador	20
United Kingdom	11	Honduras	10
Venezuela	7		

Haiti

27,750 sq. km.; 4,800,000 inhab. (+ 2.3% per year); 173 inhab.
    per sq. km.

Capital: Port-au-Prince, 270,000 inhab. (conurbation 470,000).

National currency: Gourde = $.20.

Gross domestic product in 1964: 1,910 M. gourdes ($84 per
    inhab.). Heavy preponderance of agriculture.

Annual growth rate 1958–65: approximately 2%.

Total budgetary expenditure in 1964: 155 M. gourdes.

Per capita consumption in 1964: Energy: 32 kg.

Principal products: Coffee: 35,000 tons; sisal: 25,000 tons; cocoa:
    2,500 tons; cotton, wood, bananas (United Fruit); sugar:
    70,000 tons; cattle: 650,000 head; sheep: 900,000 head;
    bauxite: 450,000 tons; copper, salt.

Foreign trade 1957, 1958*

IMPORTS CIF 1957	M Gourdes	EXPORTS FOB 1958	M Gourdes
Wheat flour	25	Coffee	157
Cotton articles	29	Sisal	28
Petroleum products	11	Cocoa	7
Automobiles (insufficiently significant statitistics)	8	Sugar	4
Total	191	U.S.A. Total	211
PRINCIPAL SUPPLIERS 1957		PRINCIPAL BUYERS 1958	
U.S.A.	119	U.S.A.	104
Canada	11	Belgium-Luxembourg	38
Curaçao	9	Italy	37
West Germany	8	France	8
United Kingdom	7	Netherlands	7

* No more recent figures available.

Mexico

1,972,500 sq. km.; 42.5 M. inhab. (+ 3.3% per year); 21.5 inhab. per sq. km.

Capital: Mexico City, 3.5 M. inhab.

Principal cities: Guadalajara, 1.05 M. inhab.; Monterrey, 850,000. Six other cities of more than 100,000 inhab.

National currency: Peso = $.08.

Gross domestic product in 1965: 245 billion pesos ($460 per inhab.). Agriculture: 17%; all industries: 32%.

Annual growth rate 1958–65: 5.6% approximately.

Total budgetary expenditure in 1965: 17.4 billion pesos.

Per capita consumption in 1964: Energy: 1,029 kg.; steel: 63 kg.

Major products: Maize: 8.5 M. tons; tobacco: 70,000 tons; cotton: 550,000 tons; coffee: 150,000 tons; sugar: 1.9 M. tons; cattle: 30 M. tons; silver: 1,300 tons (first in the world); crude oil: 16.5 M. tons; natural gas: 14,000 M. cubic meters; iron ore: 1.5 M. tons; antimony ore: 4,800 tons (fifth in the world); lead ore: 170,000 tons; zinc ore: 240,-000 tons; copper, gold, manganese, mercury, tin; steel: 2.4 M. tons; cement: 4.5 M. tons; various industries.

Foreign trade 1965

IMPORTS CIF	M Pesos	EXPORTS FOB	M Pesos
Food, animals, beverages, tobacco	875	Raw cotton	2,652
Crude materials	1,826	Maize	965
Electric energy	471	Silver, copper, lead, raw zinc	950
Chemicals	3,124	Coffee	937
Manuf. goods	2,330	Raw sugar	732
Machinery, transp. equip.	9,675	Fresh and dried vegetables	582
Misc. manuf. goods	1,062	Fresh fish	580
		Non-ferrous minerals and concentrates	545
		Wheat	521
Total	19,496	Total	14,280
PRINCIPAL SUPPLIERS		PRINCIPAL BUYERS	
U.S.A.	12,815	U.S.A.	8,013
West Germany	1,526	Japan	1,015
United Kingdom	670	Poland	725
France	606	West Germany	436
Italy	556	Switzerland	337
Japan	489	U.A.R.	256

Peru

1,285,000 sq. km.; 12 M. inhab. (+3% per year); 9.3 inhab.
  per sq. km.
Capital: Lima, 1.8 M. inhab.
Principal cities: Callao, 210,000; Arequipa, 200,000.
National currency: Sol = $.038.
Gross domestic product in 1965: Approximately 116 billion soles
  ($370 per inhab.). Agriculture: 20%; mines: 7%; indus-
  tries: 18%.
Annual growth rate 1958–65: 6.4%.
Total budgetary expenditure in 1964: 17.4 billion soles.
Per capita consumption in 1964: Energy: 602 kg.; steel: 24 kg.
Major products: Fish: 9 M. tons (first in the world for industrial
  fishing for fish meal); cotton: 160,000 tons; sugar: 780,000
  tons; iron ore: 4.3 M. tons; copper: 180,000 tons; lead:
  150,000 tons; silver: 1,150 tons; zinc: 200,000 tons; antimony, gold, mercury, molybdenum, tungsten.

Foreign trade 1963, 1965

IMPORTS CIF 1963	M Soles	EXPORTS FOB 1963	M Soles
Food, animals, beverages, tobacco	2,437	Non-ferrous metals	3,198
Crude materials	474	Livestock food (fish meal)	2,866
Coke, coal, petroleum prods.	463	Textile fibers	2,779
Chemicals	1,504	Metallic minerals	2,048
Manuf. goods	2,893	Sugar	1,738
Machinery, transp. equip.	6,325		
Misc. manuf. goods	746		
Total	14,833	Total	14,508
PRINCIPAL SUPPLIERS 1965		**PRINCIPAL BUYERS 1965**	
U.S.A.	7,780	U.S.A.	6,055
West Germany	2,291	West Germany	2,246
Japan	1,397	Japan	1,644
Argentina	1,320	Netherlands	1,631
United Kingdom	1,017	United Kingdom	1,038
		Belgium-Luxembourg	895
Total	19,562	Total	17,897

Uruguay

187,000 sq. km.; 2,800,000 inhab. (+ 1.4% per year); 14.6
inhab. per sq. km.

Capital: Montevideo, 1,250,000 inhab.

Principal cities: Paysandú, Salto, 55,000 inhab.

National currency: Peso = $.017 (end of 1965). End of 1967:
$1.00 = 200 pesos.

Gross domestic product in 1965: Approximately 110 billion pesos
($600 per inhab.). Agriculture: 15%; all industries: 24%.

Annual growth rate 1958–65: Approximately 0%.

Current external debt in 1965: Approximately $450 M.

Per capita consumption in 1964: Energy: 830 kg.; steel: 31 kg.

Major products: Cattle: 9.3 M. head; sheep: 22 M. head; meat:
350,000 tons; wool: 85,000 tons; flax seed: 75,000 tons;
sunflowers, groundnuts; wheat: 600,000 tons; potatoes, rice.
Electrical energy power installed: 460,000 kw; food industries, hide and leather.

Foreign trade 1965

IMPORTS CIF	M $U.S.	EXPORTS FOB	M $U.S.
		Wool, greasy	62
		Wool, washed	8
		Wool worsted tops	21
(Incomplete and insignificant figures)		Beef	44
		Lamb	7
		Meat extract	5
		Raw hides and skins	5
		Wheat	5
Total	151	Total	191
PRINCIPAL SUPPLIERS		PRINCIPAL BUYERS	
U.S.A.	20	U.S.A.	32
West Germany	18	United Kingdom	31
United Kingdom	15	Netherlands	18
Brazil	13	West Germany	16
Venezuela	13	Spain	15
Argentina	9	Italy	14

Venezuela

912,000 sq. km.; 9.1 M. inhab. (+ 3.4% per year); 10 inhab. per sq. km.

Capital: Caracas: 1.7 M. inhab.

Principal cities: Maracaibo, 490,000 inhab.; Barquisimeto, 230,-000; San Cristobal, 125,000; Cuidad Guayana, 100,000 (increasing rapidly).

National currency: Bolivar = $.222.

Gross domestic product in 1965: 38 billion bolivars ($950 per inhab. approx.). Agriculture: 8%; crude oil and refineries: 28%; industry: 12%.

Annual growth rate 1958–65: 5.3%.

Total budgetary expenditure in 1965: 7 billion bolivars.

Direct American investment: More than $3 billion.

Per capita consumption in 1964: Energy: 3,000 kg.; steel: 119 kg.

Major products: Crude oil: 180 M. tons (third in the world, largest exporter); natural gas: 6.3 billion cubic meters; iron ore: 11 M. tons; gold: 1,050 kg.; diamonds, manganese, nickel; refined oil: about 60 M. tons; steel: 700,000 tons; electric energy power installed: more than 2 M. kw; metal conversion, textile and food industries.

Foreign trade 1965

IMPORTS CIF	M Bolivares	EXPORTS FOB	M Bolivares
Food, beverages, tobacco	607	Crude oil	7,862
Crude materials	258	Refined petroleum products	3,367
Manufactured goods	541	Iron ore	606
Chemicals	1,224		
Machinery, transp. equip.	2,383		
Misc. manufactured goods	445		
Total	5,590	Total	12,076
PRINCIPAL SUPPLIERS		**PRINCIPAL BUYERS**	
U.S.A.	2,885	U.S.A.	4,515
West Germany	485	Netherland Antilles	2,874
Canada	360	Canada	1,153
United Kingdom	333	United Kingdom	962
Japan	297	Trinidad	642
Italy	288		

Burma

678,000 sq. km.; 25.5 M. inhab. (+ 2.9% per year); 37.5 inhab. per sq. km.

Capital: Rangoon, approximately 1 M. inhab.

Principal cities: Mandalay, approximately 250,000 inhab.; Moulmein, approximately 130,000.

National currency: Kyat = $.21.

National revenue in 1964: 6.59 billion kyats.

Gross domestic product in 1964: 7.7 billion kyats ($65 per inhab.). Agriculture: 33%; all industries: 16%.

Annual growth rate 1958–64: 4.5%.

Total budgetary expenditure in 1964: 1,150 M. kyats; 1966: 1,647 M. kyats.

Per capita consumption in 1964: Energy: 59 kg.

Major products: Rice: 7.6 M. tons; groundnuts: 375,000 tons; rubber, sesame, tobacco, millet, teak; fish: 360,000 tons; tungsten concentrate: 350 tons (production declining); tin concentrate: 900 tons; crude oil: 560,000 tons.

Foreign trade 1964

IMPORTS CIF	M Kyats	EXPORTS FOB	M Kyats
Food, beverages, tobacco	118	Rice	726
Crude materials	70	Oilseed cakes	59
Coal, coke and petroleum prods.	53	Raw cotton	26
Animal and vegetable oils		Natural rubber	15
and fats	216	Silver	9
Chemicals	106		
Manuf. goods	450		
Machinery, transp. equip.	235		
Misc. manuf. goods	44		
Total	1,293	Total	1,123
PRINCIPAL SUPPLIERS		PRINCIPAL BUYERS	
Japan	221	Indonesia	158
China	151	Ceylon	126
United Kingdom	123	United Kingdom	100
U.S.A.	122	India	88
Netherlands	77	China	80
Pakistan	77	U.S.S.R.	79

Cambodia

181,000 sq. km.; 6,500,000 inhab. (+ 3.2% per year); 36 inhab. per sq. km.

Capital: Phnom Penh, 470,000 inhab.

Principal cities: Battambang, 45,000 inhab.; Sihanoukville (port), 25,000 (developing).

National currency: Riel = $.029.

Gross domestic product in 1963: 25.5 billion riels ($120 per inhab. approx.). Agriculture: 41%; all industries: 12%.

Annual growth rate 1958–63: Approximately 5%.

Per capita consumption in 1964: Energy: 40 kg.

Principal products: Rice: 2.6 M tons; maize: 220,000 tons; groundnuts, rubber, tobacco, mulberry leaves, pepper, teak; fish: 160,000 tons.

Foreign trade 1965

IMPORTS CIF	M Riels	EXPORTS FOB	M Riels
Food, animals, tobacco	205	Rice	1,817
Coal, coke, petroleum		Rubber	1,228
and products	262	Maize	178
Chemicals	444	Oilseeds	111
Manuf. goods	1,503	Pepper and pimentos	70
Machinery, transp. equip.	929		
Misc. manuf. goods	187		
Total	3,603	Total	3,690
PRINCIPAL SUPPLIERS		PRINCIPAL BUYERS	
France	723	France	709
Japan	611	Singapore	541
China	492	Former French West Africa	479
United Kingdom	183	Hong Kong	277
Czechoslovakia	181	China	228
West Germany	157	Philippines	199

Ceylon

65,600 sq. km.; 11,500,000 inhab. (+ 2.6% per year); 175 inhab. per sq. km.

Capital: Colombo, 550,000 inhab.

Principal cities: Jaffna, 100,000 inhab.; Kandy, 80,000; Galle, 75,000.

National currency: Rupee = $.209. (Since November 1967 = $.168.)

National revenue in 1964: 6.6 billion rupees.

Gross domestic product in 1964: 7.3 billion rupees ($138 per inhab.). Agriculture: 46%; all industries: 7%.

Annual growth rate 1958–64: 3.4%.

Total budgetary expenditure in 1964: 1,880 M. rupees; 1966: 2,234 M. rupees.

Per capita consumption in 1964: Energy: 98 kg.; steel: 7 kg.

Major products: Tea: 220,000 tons (second in the world); rubber: 110,000 tons (fourth in the world); rice: 1.05 M. tons (insufficient for the population); cocoa nuts, cocoa, tobacco, cinnamon, graphite, kaolin, precious stones.

Foreign trade 1965

IMPORTS CIF	M Rupees	EXPORTS FOB	M Rupees
Food, animals	597	Tea	1,210
Crude materials	43	Rubber	304
Coal, petroleum and prods.	120	Coconut oil	142
Chemicals	153	Coconuts	82
Manufactured goods	335	Hard fibers	50
Machinery, transp. equipment	177	Copra	49
Misc. manufactured goods	34	Spices	33
Total	1,474	Total	1,916
PRINCIPAL SUPPLIERS		**PRINCIPAL BUYERS**	
United Kingdom	264	United Kingdom	505
India	134	China	172
China	114	U.S.A.	146
Japan	111	Australia	100
U.S.S.R.	100	U.S.S.R.	97
Australia	94	South Africa	92
Burma	74		

India

3,046,000 sq. km.; 1967: approximately 500 M. inhab. (+ 2.3%
per year); 164 inhab. per sq. km.

Capital: New Delhi, 325,000 inhab.

Principal cities: Calcutta, 4,900,000 inhab.; Bombay, 4,800,000;
Delhi, 2,800,000; Madras, 2 M.; Bangalore, 1,405,000;
Ahmedabad, 1,430,000.

National currency: Rupee = $.209 = 0.0747 pounds sterling.

Gross domestic product in 1965: approximately 220 billion rupees
($90 per inhab. approx.). Agriculture: 50%; all industries
and construction: 18%.

Annual growth rate 1958–65: approximately 3.8%.

Total budgetary expenditure 1965 (Union and States): 59.3 billion
rupees.

Per capita consumption in 1964: Energy: 161 kg.; steel: 16 kg.

Major products: Tea: 370,000 tons (first in the world); groundnuts: 6 M. tons; rice: 58 M. tons (second in the world);
tobacco: 350,000 tons; cotton: 1.1 M. tons (third in the
world); sugar: 2.8 M. tons; jute, pepper, hemp, flax, sesame;
coal: 63 M. tons; iron ore: 12.5 M. tons; manganese ore:
550,000 tons; mica, precious stones; steel: 6 M. tons; cotton
textiles: 4,600 M. meters (third in the world).

Foreign trade 1965

IMPORTS CIF	M Rupees	EXPORTS FOB	M Rupees
Food	3,403	Jute manufactures	1,816
Crude materials, except fuels	1,215	Other textile fabrics	949
Petroleum and products	683	Tea	1,148
Chemicals	1,048	Metallic minerals	595
Manufactured goods	2,158	Oilseed cakes	346
Machinery and transp. equip.	4,895	Fruits and vegetables	333
Misc. manufactured goods	186	Heather	282
		Mineral products	166
		Diamonds and precious stones	148
		Iron and steel	126
Total	13,940	Total	8,056
PRINCIPAL SUPPLIERS		**PRINCIPAL BUYERS**	
U.S.A.	5,256	U.S.A.	1,472
United Kingdom	1,491	United Kingdom	1,455
West Germany	1,369	U.S.S.R.	929
U.S.S.R.	825	Japan	569
Japan	792	U.A.R.	271

Indonesia

1,492,000 sq. km.; 107 M. inhab. (+ 2.2% per year); 70 inhab. per sq. km.

Capital: Djakarta, 3 M. inhab.

Principal cities: Surabaja, 1.05 M. inhab.; Bandung, 1 M.; Semarang, 540,000.

National currency: Rupiah = ? (official conversion rate: 1 rupiah = $.0222).

Gross domestic product in 1965: approximately $8,900 M. ($85 per inhab. approx.). In 1959, agriculture: 56%; all industries: 10%.

Per capita consumption in 1964: Energy: 108 kg.; steel: 2 kg.

Major products: Rubber: 650,000 tons (second in the world); groundnuts: 400,000 tons; rice: 12 M. tons; tea: 45,000 tons; soya: 400,000 tons; sugar: 700,000 tons; oil seeds, tobacco, coffee; fisheries: 950,000 tons; crude oil: 23 M. tons; tin concentrate: 17,000 tons (fourth in the world).

Foreign trade 1962, 1965

IMPORTS CIF 1962	M Rupiahs	EXPORTS FOB 1965	M Rupiahs
Food, animals, tobacco	3,673	Crude oil and pet prod.	12,237
Crude materials	460	Rubber	9,472
Coal, coke, petroleum prods.	1,824	Tin and concentrates	1,706
Chemicals	3,447	Coffee	1,421
Manufactured goods	10,338	Palm oil	1,228
Machinery, transp. equip.	8,304	Raw tobacco	862
Misc. manufactured goods	815	Copra	807
		Tea	760
Total	29,133	Total	31,795
PRINCIPAL SUPPLIERS 1962		**PRINCIPAL BUYERS 1962**	
Japan	6,082	Singapore	6,576
U.S.A.	5,253	United Kingdom	4,872
West Germany	3,356	U.S.A.	4,352
United Kingdom	2,483	Malaysia	2,687
India	695	Japan	1,845
		U.S.S.R.	1,569

Iran

1,648,000 sq. km.; 24 M. inhab. (+ 2.5% per year); 14.5 inhab. per sq. km.

Capital: Tehran, 2.5 M. inhab.

Principal cities: Tabriz, 400,000 inhab.; Isfahan, 270,000; Meshed, 260,000; Abadan, 240,000; Shiraz, 240,000.

National currency: Rial = $.0132.

Gross domestic product in 1965: 480 billion rials ($265 per inhab.). Agriculture: 30%; all industries: 29%.

Annual growth rate 1958–65: approximately 5.5%.

Total budgetary expenditure in 1965: 75 billion rials.

Per capita consumption in 1964: Energy: 386 kg.; steel: 23 kg.

Major products: Crude oil: 84 M. tons (sixth in the world); cotton: 115,000 tons; rice, tea, tobacco; cattle: approximately 35 M. head; carpets; refined petroleum products: approximately 20 M. tons; cotton industry.

Foreign trade 1964

IMPORTS CIF	M Rials	EXPORTS FOB	M Rials
Food, beverages, tobacco, animals	7,047	Crude oil	64,550
Crude materials	2,956	Petroleum products	19,018
Animal and vegetable oils		Cotton	2,643
and fats	1,121	Tapestries, etc.	2,425
Chemicals	6,440	Raw hides and skins	1,024
Manuf. goods	14,365		
Machinery, transp. equip.	16,765		
Misc. manuf. goods	1,796		
Total	50,669	Total	94,964
PRINCIPAL SUPPLIERS		**PRINCIPAL BUYERS**	
West Germany	10,188	Japan	14,747
U.S.A.	8,568	United Kingdom	12,975
United Kingdom	7,275	India	6,591
Japan	3,352	U.S.A.	6,039
U.S.S.R.	2,430	France	5,890
France	2,243	South Africa	5,160

Iraq

449,000 sq. km.; 7,300,000 inhab. (+ 1.8% per year); 16 inhab.
per sq. km.

Capital: Baghdad, 450,000 inhab.

Principal cities: Basra, 350,000 inhab.; Mosul, 190,000; Kirkuk,
130,000.

National currency: Dinar = $2.80.

Gross domestic product in 1964: 750 M. dinars ($290 per inhab.
approx.). Agriculture: 16%; products of the sub-soil: 37%;
industry: 10%.

Annual growth rate 1958–64: 7%.

Total budgetary expenditure in 1964: 203 M. dinars.

Per capita consumption in 1964: Energy: 666 kg.; steel: 28 kg.

Major products: Crude oil: 65 M. tons (seventh in the world):
dates: the world's major producer; cattle: 9.5 M. head; rice,
cotton, tobacco.

Foreign trade 1965

IMPORTS CIF	M Dinars	EXPORTS FOB	M Dinars
(Incomplete and insignificant information)		Crude oil	294
		Dates	6
Total	161	Total	312
PRINCIPAL SUPPLIERS		PRINCIPAL BUYERS	
U.S.A.	19	United Kingdom	50
United Kingdom	18	France	49
West Germany	15	Italy	40
U.S.S.R.	12	Netherlands	25
Japan	9	West Germany	23
Czechoslovakia	9	Japan	22

Malaya[1]

131,300 sq. km.; 8.3 M. inhab., of which 38% are Chinese
(+ 3.1% per year); 64 inhab. per sq. km.

Capital: Kuala Lumpur, 500,000 inhab.

Principal cities: George Town, 250,000 inhab.; Ipoh, 140,000.

National currency: Malayan dollar = $.326 U.S. (devalued in
.November 1967).

Gross domestic product in 1965: 7,230 Mal. $ ($290 U.S. per
inhab.). Agriculture: 31%; mines: 9%; industries: 9%.

Annual growth rate 1958–65: approximately 5.5%.

Total budgetary expenditure in 1965: approximately 1,600 M.
Mal. $.

Per capita consumption in 1964: Energy: 339 kg.; steel: 43 kg.

Major products: Rubber: 830,000 tons (first in the world); palm
oil: 120,000 tons; wood, cocoa nuts, pineapples; tin concentrate: 61,000 tons (first in the world); iron ore: 4 M. tons;
bauxite: 470,000 tons.

---

[1] Malaya itself, not the Federation.

Foreign trade 1965

IMPORTS CIF	M Malayan $	EXPORTS FOB	M Malayan $
Food, animals, beverages, tobacco	675	Rubber	1,369
Crude materials	229	Tin and alloys	865
Coke, coal, petroleum products	174	Iron ore	161
Chemicals	217	Palm oil	106
Manufactured goods	510	Wood	92
Machinery, transp. equip.	580		
Misc. manufactured goods	156		
Total	2,608	Total	3,103
PRINCIPAL SUPPLIERS		**PRINCIPAL BUYERS**	
United Kingdom	532	Singapore	650
Japan	300	U.S.A.	548
Thailand	275	Japan	394
Singapore	274	United Kingdom	251
China	174	U.S.S.R.	226
Australia	160	West Germany	107
		Italy	102

Pakistan

946,700 sq. km.; 105 M. inhab. (+ 2.1% per year); 118 inhab. per sq. km.

Capital: Rawalpindi, 420,000 inhab. (West Pakistan).

Principal cities in West Pakistan: Karachi, 2 M. inhab.; Lahore, 1.35 M.; Hyderabad, 450,000; Multan, 380,000; Peshawar, 230,000. *East Pakistan:* Dacca, 580,000; Chittagong, 380,- 000; Khulna, 140,000.

National currency: Rupee = $.208.

Gross domestic product in 1965: 52.8 billion rupees ($107 per inhab.). Agriculture: 48%; all industries: 12%.

Annual growth rate 1958–65: approximately 5%.

Total budgetatry expenditure in 1965 (Central Government & States): 11.5 billion rupees.

Per capita consumption in 1964: Energy: 86 kg.; steel: 11 kg.

Major products: Rice: 18 M. tons (third in the world); wheat: 4.2 M. tons; cotton: 400,000 tons; tea: 28,000 tons; tobacco: 100,000 tons; jute: the leading world producer in competition with India; cattle: 35 M. head; iron ore; natural gas: 1,800 M. cubic meters; cotton thread: 240,000 tons; major artisan products; steel works under construction.

Foreign trade 1965

IMPORTS CIF	M Rupees	EXPORTS FOB	M Rupees
Food, beverages, tobacco	753	Jute	847
Crude materials	168	Raw cotton	307
Coal, coke, petroleum prods.	165	Wool	72
Animal and vegetable oils and fats	237	Textile yarns, fabrics, etc.	721
		Rice	119
Chemicals	463	Leather	67
Manuf. goods	1,150	Fish	60
Machinery, transp. equip.	1,884	Raw hides and skins	37
Misc. manuf. goods	145		
Total	4,967	Total	2,515
PRINCIPAL SUPPLIERS		**PRINCIPAL BUYERS**	
U.S.A.	1,737	United Kingdom	338
United Kingdom	736	U.S.A.	226
West Germany	699	China	205
Japan	489	India	138
Italy	166	Japan	114
		Belgium-Luxembourg	112
		Hong Kong	90

Philippines

300,000 sq. km.; 33.5 M. inhab. (+ 3.3% per year); 111 inhab. per sq. km.

Capital: Quezon, 450,000 inhab.

Principal cities: Manila, 1.25 M. inhab.; Cebu, 280,000; Davao, 260,000; Iloilo, 170,000.

National currency: Peso = $.256.

Gross domestic product in 1965: 20,400 M. pesos ($160 per inhab.). Agriculture: 34%; all industries: 20%.

Annual growth rate 1958–65: 4.5%.

Total budgetary expenditure in 1965: 2,035 M. pesos.

Per capita consumption in 1964: Energy: 203 kg.; steel: 22 kg.

Major products: Rice: 4 M. tons; maize: 1.3 M. tons; copra: 1 M. tons; tobacco: 55,000 tons; Manila hemp: 100,000 tons; sugar: 1.7 M. tons; timber: 7 M. cubic meters; fish: 650,000 tons; chrome ore: 160,000 tons (fourth in the world); iron ore: 800,000 tons; copper ore: 60,000 tons; gold: 13,000 kg. (eighth in the world); silver, mercury, molybdenum, food and textile industries.

Foreign trade 1965

IMPORTS FOB	M $U.S.	EXPORTS FOB	M $U.S.
Food, beverages, tobacco	167	Copra	170
Crude materials	36	Sugar	156
Petroleum and products	73	Wood	154
Chemicals	76	Metallic minerals	79
Manuf. goods	c. 200	Coconut oil	67
Machinery, transp. equip.	262	Fruits and vegetables	35
Misc. manuf. goods	22	Wood products	27
Total	835	Total	794
PRINCIPAL SUPPLIERS		**PRINCIPAL BUYERS**	
U.S.A.	292	U.S.A.	381
Japan	201	Japan	208
West Germany	37	Netherlands	77
United Kingdom	33	West Germany	30
Burma	30	Taiwan	12
Canada	26	Sweden	11

Saudi Arabia

2,253,000 sq. km.; 6.9 M. inhab. (+ 1.7% per year); 3.7 inhab.
per sq. km.

Capital: Riyadh, 325,000 inhab.

Principal cities: Jidda (port), 240,000 inhab.; Mecca, 220,000
and Medina, 60,000 (holy cities).

National currency: Riyal = $.22.

Gross domestic product in 1965: approximately 3.98 billion riyals
($130 per inhab. approx.).

Per capita consumption in 1964: Energy: 320 kg.; steel: 23 kg.

Major products: Crude oil: 110 M. tons. Apart from oil, an extremely poor economy. Minor production of coffee, cotton,
cereals. Dates, cattle, and camels. Refined petroleum products: about one-sixth of the crude oil extracted.

Foreign trade 1965 (5-12-64/4-30-65)

IMPORTS CIF	M Riyals	EXPORTS FOB	M Riyals
Food, animals, beverages, tobacco	296	Crude oil	5,002
		Refined petroleum prods.	949
Crude materials, chemicals, manufactured goods	411		
Electric and other machinery	193		
Automobiles	247		
Misc. manuf. goods	35		
Total	1,575	Total	5,968

PRINCIPAL SUPPLIERS		PRINCIPAL BUYERS	
U.S.A.	337	Japan	1,196
United Kingdom	147	Italy	722
Japan	125	U.S.A.	460
Lebanon	114	Bahrain	435
West Germany	102	West Germany	315
Italy	98	France	274

South Korea

98,500 sq. km.; 28.5 M. inhab. (+ 2.8% per year); 290 inhab.
   per sq. km.

Capital: Seoul, 3,100,000 inhab.

Principal cities: Pusan, 1,350,000 inhab.; Taegu, 750,000.

National currency: Won = $.0037.

Gross domestic product in 1965: 760 billion won ($100 per
   inhab. approx.). Agriculture: 41%; all industries 21%.

Annual growth rate 1958–65: 6%.

Total budgetary expenditure in 1965: 96 billion won.

Per capita consumption in 1964: Energy: 410 kg.

Major products: Rice: 4 M. tons; barley: 900,000 tons; wheat;
   fish: 500,000 tons; coal: 9.5 M. tons; molybdenum: 120
   tons; tungsten: 3,600 tons (fourth in the world); industrialization beginning.

Foreign trade 1965

IMPORTS CIF	M $U.S.	EXPORTS FOB	M $U.S.
Food	64	Textile, yarns, fabrics, etc.	26
Crude materials	110	Clothing	21
Coal, coke, petroleum		Metalliferous ores	18
and products	31	Veneers, plywood boards, etc.	18
Chemicals	103	Iron and steel	13
Manuf. goods	71	Misc. manuf. goods	9
Machinery and transp. equip.	60	Fish	7
Misc. manuf. goods	7		
Total	450	Total	175
PRINCIPAL SUPPLIERS		**PRINCIPAL BUYERS**	
U.S.A.	182	U.S.A.	62
Japan	167	Japan	44
West Germany	16	South Vietnam	15
Philippines	11	Hong Kong	11
Taiwan	10		

Syria

185,000 sq. km.; 5,500,000 inhab. (+ 3.2% per year); 30 inhab. per sq. km.

Capital: Damascus, 575,000 inhab.

Principal cities: Aleppo, 550,000 inhab.; Homs, 360,000; Hama, 220,000; Latakia, 160,000.

National currency: Syrian pound = $.262.

Gross domestic product in 1965: approximately 4,150 Syrian pounds ($200 per inhab.). Agriculture: 37%; all industries: 13%.

Annual growth rate 1958–65: approximately 6%.

Total budgetary expenditure in 1965: 516 M. Syrian pounds.

Per capita consumption in 1964: Energy: 351 kg.; steel: 28 kg.

Major products: Wheat: 1.2 M. tons; barley: 700,000 tons; cotton: 170,000 tons; silk production, declining; cattle: 6 M. head; foodstuffs cultivated; no energy or mineral resources; industries transforming products of the soil.

Foreign trade 1965

IMPORTS CIF	M £ Syrian	EXPORTS FOB	M £ Syrian
Food, animals, beverages, tobacco	174	Raw cotton	285
Crude materials	60	Barley	50
Coke, coal, petroleum		Live sheep, lambs, goats	38
and products	83	Dry vegetables	33
Chemicals	93	Oilseed cakes	33
Manufactured goods	240	Textile yarns and fabrics	29
Machinery, transp. equip.	126	Wool	27
Misc. manufactured goods	29	Cottonseed oil	16
Total	810	Total	641
PRINCIPAL SUPPLIERS		**PRINCIPAL BUYERS**	
West Germany	94	Lebanon	143
United Kingdom	69	U.S.S.R.	66
Iraq	67	China	64
U.S.A.	55	Italy	40
France	51	Romania	39
Italy	46	France	35

Thailand

514,000 sq. km.; 31.5 M. inhab. (+ 3.0% per year); 60 inhab. per. sq. km.

Capital: Bangkok, 1.8 M. inhab. (conurbation).

Principal cities: Nakhon Ratchasima, 55,000 inhab.; Lampang, 45,000.

National currency: Baht = $.048.

Gross domestic product in 1965: approximately 80 billion bahts ($125 per inhab. approx.). Agriculture: 33%; all industries: 15%.

Annual growth rate 1958–65: approximately 6%.

Total budgetary expenditure in 1965: 12.8 billion bahts.

Per capita consumption in 1964: Energy: 106 kg.; steel: 13 kg.

Major products: Rice: 10 M. tons (fourth in the world); maize; rubber: 200,000 tons (third in the world); sugar: 160,000 tons; fish: 550,000 tons; copra, cotton, tobacco, teak, jute; tin concentrate: 15,800 tons (fifth in the world); antimony ore: 1,800 tons; iron, tungsten, manganese ores; food and textile industries.

Foreign trade 1965

IMPORTS CIF	M Bahts	EXPORTS FOB	M Bahts
Food, beverages, tobacco	1,073	Rice	4,376
Crude materials	466	Rubber	2,000
Coal, coke, petroleum and		Jute	1,121
prods.	1,357	Maize	980
Chemicals	1,649	Tin ore and concs.	766
Manuf. goods	4,603	Vegetables	470
Machinery, transp. equip.	4,462	Tin	400
Misc. manuf. goods	894	Oilseeds	213
Total	15,081	Total	12,750
PRINCIPAL SUPPLIERS		**PRINCIPAL BUYERS**	
Japan	4,806	Japan	2,405
U.S.A.	2,931	Malaysia	1,903
United Kingdom	1,317	Hong Kong	859
West Germany	1,306	U.S.A.	841
Netherlands	497	Singapore	808
Hong Kong	390	West Germany	641

Turkey

780,600 sq. km.; 33.5 M. inhab. (+ 2.8% per year); 43 inhab. per sq. km.

Capital: Ankara, 750,000 inhab.

Principal cities: Istanbul, 1,700,000 inhab.; Izmir (Smyrna), 400,000; Adana, 250,000; Bursa, 240,000.

National currency: Lira = $.11.

Gross domestic product in 1965: 79.5 billion lira ($280 per inhab.). Agriculture: 36%; all industries: 18%.

Annual growth rate 1958–65: approximately 4.6%.

Total budgetary expenditure in 1965: 14,420 M. lira.

Per capita consumption in 1964: Energy: 333 kg.; steel: 26 kg.

Major products: Wheat: 9 M. tons; tobacco: 170,000 tons (fifth in the world); cotton: 325,000 tons (eighth in the world); citrus, nuts, wine, tea; olive oil: 120,000 tons (fourth in the world); sheep: 33 M. head; cattle: 13 M. head; charcoal: 4.5 M. tons; lignite: 3 M. tons; crude oil: 900,000 tons; chrome ore: 180,000 tons (fifth in the world); iron ore: 600,000 tons; antimony ore: 1,500 tons; copper ore, mercury, manganese. ore; steel: 400,000 tons; cement: 3 M. tons; hydroelectric potential; textile industries (100,000 tons of cotton thread), and chemical industries.

Foreign trade 1965

IMPORTS CIF	M Lira	EXPORTS FOB	M Lira
Food, live animals	270	Raw cotton	884
Crude materials	398	Raw tobacco	806
Petroleum and products	518	Edible nuts	618
Chemicals	819	Dried grapes and figs	256
Manuf. goods	1,051	Oilseed cakes	160
Machinery, transp. equip.	1,941	Live sheep and bovines	156
Misc. manuf. goods	156	Copper and alloys	155
		Wood	115
		Olive oil	102
Total	5,193	Total	4,130

PRINCIPAL SUPPLIERS		PRINCIPAL BUYERS	
U.S.A.	1,459	U.S.A.	736
West Germany	762	West Germany	643
United Kingdom	503	United Kingdom	372
Italy	335	Italy	270
France	194	Belgium-Luxembourg	207
Saudi Arabia	178	Lebanon	190